10,95

MOHIN

D1267368

BRITISH LABOUR
AND HITLER'S WAR

BRITISH LABOUR AND HITLER'S WAR

T. D. Burridge

ANDRE DEUTSCH

First published 1976 by
André Deutsch Limited
105 Great Russell Street London WC1

Copyright © 1976 by T. D. Burridge
All rights reserved

Printed in Great Britain by
Ebenezer Baylis & Son Ltd
The Trinity Press, Worcester, and London

ISBN 0 233 96714 1

Contents

Acknowledgements

FINANCIAL support for the research on which this book is based was generously provided by the Canada Council, the Government of Quebec and the Faculty of Graduate Studies at McGill University through the McConnell Foundation. The Canada Council also facilitated the preparation of the book. None of these bodies has any responsibility for the views expressed here, which only enhances my sense of indebtedness to them.

I am most grateful for the services rendered me by the archivists, librarians and their assistants at Balliol College; the Beaverbrook Library; the Bodleian Library; Churchill College; the Brynmor Jones Library at the University of Hull; the Labour Party Library; the London School of Economics; McGill University; the Public Records Office, London; St Antony's College; Sir George Williams University; and University College, Oxford.

Mr Nigel Nicolson was kind enough to allow me to see his father's unpublished diaries and I have had the privilege of corresponding with and discussing some of the events and personalities mentioned in the following pages with the Right Honourable P. J. Noel-Baker. Mrs J. L. Middleton, widow of a former general secretary of the Labour Party and a political activist in her own right, has courteously responded to my queries.

Dr A. Fitzpatrick, Mr A. Krishtalka, Professor E. E. McCullough and Mrs Marilyn Sims read the manuscript; I have profited considerably from their suggestions. Mrs Jennifer Fowler, also of Montreal, has coped admirably with my handwriting; her secretarial expertise has greatly eased the manuscript's preparation.

The book originated as a Ph.D. thesis which was supervised by Dr R. Vogel, Dean of Arts at McGill University; he also read the manuscript. To him I owe a special word of thanks; his constructive criticism and advice have been invaluable.

However, it has been my wife who has had to live with me while

7

both thesis and book were being researched and written. Apart from her general forbearance, she has been directly helpful in ways too numerous to detail.

After such assistance, the shortcomings which remain must clearly be mine alone.

I acknowledge with thanks permission to quote from
(a) the following unpublished material:

C. R. Attlee, *Papers*, University College, Oxford.
Cabinet, Chiefs of Staff and Prime Minister's Office, *Papers, 1939–45*, HMSO.
Hugh Dalton, *Diaries and Papers*, British Library of Political and Economic Science (LSE).
Harold Nicolson, *Diaries*, Mr N. Nicolson, Balliol College and Collins.
The Labour Party, *Documents, Minutes and Papers*.

(b) the following published works:

L. S. Amery, *My Political Life*, vol. III: *The Unforgiving Years*. Hutchinson.
C. R. Attlee, *Clem Attlee*. Panther Record, Granada Publishing Co.
C. R. Attlee, *et al. Churchill by his Contemporaries: An Observer Appreciation*. Hodder and Stoughton and *The Observer*, London.
J. Braunthal, *Need Germany Survive?* Victor Gollancz.
Angus Calder, *The People's War: Britain, 1939–45*. Jonathan Cape.
W. S. Churchill, *The Second World War*, vols. II and IV. Cassell.
Hugh Dalton, *Hitler's War: Before and After*. Penguin.
Hugh Dalton, *Memoirs, 1931–45: The Fateful Years*. Frederick Muller.
D. Dilks, ed., *The Diaries of Sir Alexander Cadogan, 1938–45*. Cassell.
Piers Dixon, *Double Diplomat: The Life of Sir Pierson Dixon, Don and Diplomat*. Hutchinson.
Sir Anthony Eden, *The Eden Memoirs: The Reckoning*. Cassell.
Michael Foot, *Aneurin Bevan: A Biography*, vol. I: *1897–1945*. MacGibbon and Kee (Granada Publishing Co.).
C. Geyer, *Hitler's New Order: Kaiser's Old Order*. Hutchinson.
C. Geyer and W. Loeb, *Gollancz in German Wonderland*. Hutchinson.
Michael Howard, *The Mediterranean Strategy in the Second World War*. Weidenfeld and Nicolson.
Edward Hyams, *The New Statesman: The History of the First Fifty Years*. Longmans, Green.
Kingsley Martin, *Harold Laski, 1893–1950: A Biographical Memoir*. Victor Gollancz.
Herbert Morrison, *Herbert Morrison: An Autobiography*. Odhams (The Hamlyn Publishing Group).

Acknowledgements

J. F. Naylor, *Labour's International Policy: The Labour Party in the 1930s.* Weidenfeld and Nicolson.

Nigel Nicolson, ed., *Harold Nicolson: Diaries and Letters, 1939–45.* Collins.

Henry Pelling, *A History of British Trade Unionism.* Penguin.

General Sikorski Historical Institute, *Documents on Polish-Soviet Relations, 1939–45*, vol. II: *1943–45.* Heinemann.

Emanuel Shinwell, *The Labour Story: Being a History of the Labour Party.* Macdonald and James.

Lord Strang, *At Home And Abroad.* André Deutsch.

A. J. P. Taylor, *The Trouble-Makers.* Panther.

A. J. P. Taylor, *English History: 1914–45.* © 1965 Oxford University Press, and by permission of The Clarendon Press, Oxford.

A. J. P. Taylor, *Beaverbrook.* Hamish Hamilton.

A. J. P. Taylor, ed., *Lloyd George: Twelve Essays.* Hamish Hamilton.

The General Secretary, Trades Union Congress, *Report of the Proceedings of the Annual Conference, 1939–45.* TUC.

Sir Llewellyn Woodward, *British Foreign Policy in the Second World War.* HMSO.

Abbreviations

―――――

APW Committee	Armistice and Post-War Committee of the War Cabinet
EAC	European Advisory Commission
ILP	Independent Labour Party
International sub-committee	International sub-committee of the National Executive Committee of the Labour Party
NEC	National Executive Committee of the Labour Party
NCL	National Council of Labour
PLP	Parliamentary Labour Party
p.o.w.s	prisoners of war
TUC	Trades Union Congress

Introduction

THE addition of another book to the staggering quantity of literature on the Second World War demands an explanation, if not an apology. It is true that more than thirty years have passed and this does provide certain advantages. In itself, however, perspective does not suffice; much also depends upon the topic, the point of view and the availability of new material. The justification for the present study rests on all three of these factors.

My central purpose is to examine the contribution made by the Labour Party to the formulation of British foreign policy during the war. It will be contended that the Labour leadership had a primary responsibility for that policy. The Coalition government was nowhere more a political partnership than in the field of foreign affairs, which was the reason for its existence. The Labour ministers, it will be seen, were involved in this field from the beginning and, thanks to the decision of the Cabinet Office to release the *Cabinet Papers*, their precise views and contributions can now be ascertained. In particular, the frequent assumption that 'Labour had little to do with the shaping of British foreign policy during the war'[1] can be disproved.

The most important problem confronting the policy-makers was that of Germany, as it had been for the previous fifty years. This was certainly the pivotal issue for Labour and the one on which the book will concentrate. The war, the Party's formal participation in the government and the nature of the German régime constituted the severest of political tests. As a result, Labour came not only to change its collective mind about Germany but also its overall approach to international affairs. The book seeks as well, therefore, to describe that change, to see how it came about and to analyse the conflicts of Party and individual Labour opinion over the foreign policy which subsequently emerged.

To a large extent, the story of the Labour Party's approach to international affairs in the first half of the twentieth century has been one of a controversy between principles and practice, the attempt to relate 'socialist' theory to the changing realities of the international scene. In one sense this is surprising as it has become commonplace for historians to minimize the effect of ideology or doctrine on the Party's more general intellectual development. Even so, the influence of Marxist or Marx-derived ideas, particularly on the political rather than industrial wing of the Party, can hardly be denied.[2] Such influence was most pronounced in the sphere of foreign policy. Official and unofficial Labour spokesmen and protagonists rarely hesitated to claim authority for their often widely differing statements by reference to a theoretical Holy Grail.

During the final stages of the First World War the movement for a negotiated peace brought about a temporary accord over international issues between the usually disparate political and industrial segments. Afterwards, the inclusion of a well-informed and highly articulate group of middle-class *Recruits To Labour* noticeably sharpened the polemical tone of deliberations on foreign affairs.[3] And at no time was this tendency more prevalent than during the 1930s. These years were characterized by unprecedented international developments, above all the rise of Fascism. They were also years of considerable revival in Party ferment and dissent, exacerbated by the prevailing distrust of leadership[4] which followed the 'Great Betrayal' of 1931. Possibly more important in psychological terms, the period was one in which the Labour Party never appeared likely to obtain any real measure of power. When Labour finally secured an overall majority in the House of Commons, in 1945, a decisive point was reached. The true nature of the Party's attitude to foreign policy could be assessed, and great was the surprise in some quarters when the Labour government pursued a foreign policy along traditionally British rather than traditionally 'socialist' lines.[5] The Labour Party, however, was already committed to the broad direction of the policy which it had helped to produce during the war.

The outbreak of hostilities in 1939 coincided with a fundamental improvement in the Party's structural cohesion. For a variety of reasons, the decade had witnessed the elimination or discredit of every organized group within the Party which had dissented radically from the official leadership. The Independent Labour Party had reduced itself to isolation and impotence in 1931;[6] the demise of the pacifists, which had begun in 1935 with Ernest Bevin's celebrated personal onslaught on George Lansbury, was completed by the events of September 1939; the Socialist League had been expelled in 1937[7] and, with the signing of the Nazi-Soviet Pact on August 22, 1939, most of any remaining communist or fellow-travelling influence collapsed overnight.

It should be emphasized that, although clear enough in retrospect, the political significance of these developments was not so evident at the time. Nor did they mean that all attempts to organize dissent, to influence policy, or to criticize the leadership ceased during the war. Though deficient in political organization, the critics lacked neither eloquent voices nor the means of making them heard. The impact of their strictures, however, was seriously weakened in two ways. In the first place, the dissenters could not agree among themselves. Secondly, such debate as took place was circumscribed by the rank-and-file's necessary ignorance of what exactly was being advocated and decided in the war cabinet. Moreover, control of the Party had drastically changed since the 1931 débâcle. What was then left of the Parliamentary Labour Party, after the exclusion of Ramsay MacDonald and other leaders, was taken over by the Trade Union Congress and the extra-parliamentary party.[8] After the 1935 election policy-making was roughly divided between the National Council of Labour (which was dominated by Bevin and Sir Walter Citrine, the General Secretary of the TUC) and the National Executive Committee of the Party, which included the parliamentary leadership.[9] In 1940, when Clement Attlee and Bevin joined the government, Party authority became as concentrated as it had ever been. Between them, these two men united Labour's political, parliamentary and industrial sections. The official leadership was in an unassailable position, though this was not at once fully appreciated.

Equally important, the structural changes corresponded to and reflected a new sense of ideological unity. The Party as a whole was obliged to agree that the international Fascist enemy would have to be given precedence over the domestic capitalist one. For much of the previous decade there had been ambiguity or confusion over this issue.

The manifest failure of the Chamberlain government's foreign policy did more than help Labour resolve a deep-rooted question of priorities; it also thrust the Party into national pre-eminence, as the next general election was to prove. The usual, rather hackneyed argument is that Labour somehow 'matured' during the war. More accurately, the challenge of war brought to the fore in the Labour Party a maturity long residing in it, notably an otherwise unavailable expertise not now distorted by ideology. This expertise included a profound knowledge and awareness of the labour, industrial and economic aspects of foreign affairs. Indeed, the range of opinion in the Party's wartime debates on the subject better reflected the nation than did Conservative or Liberal opinion. Aneurin Bevan, Labour's chief parliamentary dissenter, was considerably more open-eyed and realistic than his counterparts had been during the 1930s.

No international question was as significant or acute as that of Germany's future; and no member of the Coalition government played a greater role in the determination of British policy towards Germany than did Labour's leader, Clement Attlee. Ernest Bevin also took an active part, especially during the last crucial years. The Foreign Secretary, of course, was influential, and Eden has told his story. But the influence of the Foreign Office was limited by the circumstance of war and coalition. Above all, the contributions of the Labour ministers have been obscured by Churchill's predominance in the implementation of policy and even more by his historical interpretation of it. This book attempts to redress the balance.

CHAPTER I

Labour and the Advent of War

SHORTLY after noon on Sunday, September 3, 1939, a visibly affected
Prime Minister informed a tense House of Commons that, for the
second time within a generation, Great Britain and Germany were at
war. The news itself hardly came as a surprise; Neville Chamberlain
had announced it on the radio earlier that morning. What exercised
the members was their sense of an impending personal and political
denouement. Nor were these presentiments falsified by the event; the
hour and the speech effectively marked finis to a political career, a
policy and, indeed, an era. 'Everything I have worked for, everything
I have hoped for, everything I have believed in during my public life
has crashed into ruins . . .'[1] Chamberlain added painfully, and even
pathetically. But the ramifications of the situation far exceeded the
Prime Minister's personal tragedy. Scarcely twenty years had elapsed
since the 'Great War'; during the intervening period, the endeavours,
the hopes and the beliefs of many individuals had been directed towards
ensuring it would not, and should not, happen again.

To no organized political group did this apply more than to the
Labour Party. Certainly no other party had more convincingly demonstrated its utter revulsion from the earlier conflict. There was one
special reason for this: some of Labour's leaders had resolutely opposed
the previous war at the time, in sharp contrast to most of their supporters. Subsequently, the Party as a whole had come to believe that
these leaders had been right. Moreover, abhorrence of the 1914–18
blood-bath vied with an almost equally strong conviction that any
repetition would be worse. Labour revived and even added to its
erstwhile reputation of being anti-war and against anything associated
with war, such as national armaments, conscription and military estab-
lishments. Though the Party never officially adopted an outright
pacifist position, a dedicated pacifist, George Lansbury, was Leader of
the Party from 1932–35. In addition, Socialist theory interpreted war

in economic terms as a clash of rival imperialisms – the last, most decadent stage of capitalism. Even towards the end of the turbulent 1930s, the Party's advocacy of the collective security doctrine owed relatively little to the idea that the possession of allies would be the best means of fighting a war. Instead, much greater emphasis was placed on the argument that a collective security policy would be the most effective way of preventing a major war.

These general ideas had appeared particularly applicable in the case of Germany. Practically no one in the Party doubted that the Versailles Treaty had been anything other than a gross injustice. Labour's apparent ambivalence, if not confusion, over Chamberlain's appeasement policy had been due – at least in part – to post-Versailles guilt, though the Party bore no responsibility for that settlement. In spite of the fact that the Labour movement as a whole witnessed the growth of German National Socialism with horror and detestation, few Labour supporters questioned the validity of certain German[2] grievances appropriated by the Nazis.

Labour's immediate reaction to the Prime Minister's announcement on that fateful September morning is thus all the more striking. For, individually and collectively, it was one of relief.

The first leading member of the Party to learn of the despatch of the British ultimatum to Germany was Hugh Dalton. His encounter late at night on September 2 with Lord Halifax, the Foreign Secretary, has often been cited[3] and his retrospective description of the incident confirms the spirit of the more dramatic accounts: 'War At Last.'[4] Dalton, it will be seen, was the outstanding exception among the Labour leadership at this time in regard to the problem of Germany in Europe. Nevertheless, it was his reaction and not that of Chamberlain which was to be widely echoed in the Party within the next few days. Addressing the Commons immediately after the Prime Minister on September 3, Arthur Greenwood (deputizing for the convalescent Attlee) declared that 'This morning we meet in an entirely different atmosphere – one of relief, one of composure, and one of resolution'.[5] Herbert Morrison, like many other Londoners, retained a vivid memory of the air-raid sirens sounding just after the expiry of the ultimatum and commented that 'It was a relief, though not a surprise, to see the civil population going to shelters or trenches not in a panic but in an orderly manner'.[6] The atmosphere at the country-cottage home of Aneurin Bevan, Party rebel and expellee, has been described by his biographer as 'A sense of relief mingled with presentiments about the unknown horrors ahead'.[7] Kingsley Martin, the editor of the Left-wing *New Statesman*, despite his strong pacifist leanings, also greeted the new situation some days later with 'A note of something like exhausted relief'.[8]

Only Lansbury – destined, as was Chamberlain, to die within a year – considered that the cause he had represented was 'apparently going down to ruins'.[9] In this surmise, Lansbury was perfectly correct. How, therefore, to account for the predominant Party mood?

It was, in the first place, a reaction to what appeared to be hesitation on the part of the government between the commencement of the German attack on Poland on September 1 and the presentation of the British ultimatum. Under the terms of the Anglo-Polish Agreement, concluded on April 6, 1939, and re-affirmed by the Anglo-Polish Mutual Assistance Treaty of August 25, 1939, Great Britain had committed itself to the defence of Polish independence. The delay in issuing the ultimatum was mainly due to poor co-ordination with the French government, who were equally committed. But this was not widely known at the time and during the final stages of the Polish crisis the Labour leadership had made its position clear. On August 23 the National Council of Labour (NCL) declared that the Labour movement stood by Britain's obligations to Poland.[10] The following day, the Party's popular organ, the *Daily Herald*, presumed to speak for the nation at large:

> . . . let no nation, [warned the paper's editorial] make the mistake of thinking that the profound criticism of the Government's past record in national and international affairs which Labour has made, and still makes, means a division in the ranks of Britain in the event of war. There will be no such division. In their determination to stand by Poland if she is attacked the leaders and members of all Parties are united.

This was not true, but on August 25 a joint meeting of all three of *Labour*'s executive bodies – the national executive committee (NEC), the general council of the Trades Union Congress (TUC), and the executive committee of the Parliamentary Labour Party (PLP), sent a 'final message of friendship and warning to the German people'.[11] The message stated that the Nazi-Soviet Pact had 'made no difference at all to the position of Britain and France. The pledges of the British government to Poland, with the approval of British Labour, stand completely unaffected.'[12] Thus the apparent delay in the despatch of the ultimatum came as a shock. Apart from the political hyperbole of the moment, the leadership had meant what it said. Moreover, it soon became evident that the leadership enjoyed the support and commanded the confidence of the rank and file. A rail strike, arranged by the National Union of Railwaymen for August 26, was called off.

A joint meeting of the NEC and the executive committee of the PLP on September 2 therefore resolved that Greenwood should make immediate representations to the Prime Minister,

> ... indicating that the two Executive Committees were prepared to support the fulfilment of the Treaty with Poland, and that the Government would be expected to announce to the House of Commons as to when, in company with the French Government, they were prepared to take action to honour the Treaty obligations to which they were committed.[13]

This was supported by a meeting of the PLP on the same day, though Dalton did note that 'Some colleagues, ... are inclined to the view that, if France won't fight, we cannot either, no matter what the terms of our treaty with the Poles may be'.[14] In the event, France did fight.

Greenwood took the strongest possible line in the Commons, demanding to know 'How long were they [the government] prepared to vacillate?'[15] After the debate he '... followed the Prime Minister to his room and told him that unless the inevitable decision for war was taken before [the Commons] met next day it would be impossible to hold the House'.[16] For Greenwood, and most other Party leaders,[17] the 'die had been cast' from the moment the German planes and tanks crossed the Polish frontier at dawn on September 1. Chamberlain's communication of that day, Greenwood publicly charged, gave 'the German Government an opportunity to withdraw'; but, in his opinion, there could be no withdrawal 'and in any event this nation is in honour bound'.[18] The act of aggression had taken place and Greenwood, on August 29, had emphasized that, so far as the Labour Party was concerned, aggression had to cease at once.[19] Further confirmation of the Party's position, if any were needed, came from the TUC's annual conference, meeting on September 4: a declaration of the general council to the effect that 'the Nazi Government must be resisted to the utmost' was passed with only two dissenting voices.[20]

But all this could simply indicate that Labour's relief at the expiry of the British ultimatum was due to a considerable swing in the Party's attitude to the Polish guarantee which had taken place at the end of August. The leadership had been seriously disturbed, originally, by the exclusion of Russia from the new policy. The chairman of the Party's annual conference, on May 29, stated that the acid test of the government's 'new-found faith in collective security' was whether they succeeded in obtaining an Anglo-Soviet-French alliance.[21] As well, the Party had been troubled by press interpretations which had stressed that 'Poland's independence rather than her territorial integrity had been guaranteed'. There had been a division of opinion among the leadership; 'some wanted to hold out for Russian inclusion, while others saw the guarantee as the first instalment of collective security, following on which every effort should be made to broaden its base'.[22] Bevan condemned the guarantee on August 24 as 'a mistake. It was militarily silly. It should have followed and not preceded negotiations with Russia.'[23]

The sum total of these opinions had remained obscure. They illustrate the difficulty historians have had in trying to assess Labour's international policy during the late 1930s; one has described it as a process of slow realization that a war would be necessary,[24] another as a period of 'upheaval, not of evolution'.[25] Indeed, just prior to the final parliamentary debate on the Polish crisis, it would have been plausible to assert that the Party had come close to admitting that there was, and had been, no real alternative to Chamberlain's earlier policy of appeasement. The debate which concluded on September 3 offered a final opportunity to make a clear political break; henceforth, Conservative policy could be presented as following Labour's. Labour could now pride itself not only on the apparent reversal of policy by the government, but also on Labour's part in bringing about that reversal.

The emotional catharsis which the Party underwent during the last few days of peace, however, was of a more profound character. It is possible to discern a distinct growth in the Party's self-confidence, and especially that of its leadership, from the onset of the war. The 'underdog' character of pre-war days – a concomitant of its well-nigh hopeless parliamentary position and the sharp, organized internal divisions – slowly but surely began to dissipate. As the international crisis deepened and the policy of the Conservative government fell apart, Labour threw off its inferiority complex. What also happened in September was that Labour's foremost ideological enemy, Fascism, became the nation's enemy as well. Emanuel Shinwell's description of Greenwood's famous response to a Conservative MP's shout of 'Speak for England' on September 2 is particularly illuminating. Shinwell – who remained on the opposition benches throughout the war – considered Greenwood's reply 'a restrained but splendid speech which destroyed for ever any lingering beliefs from the past that the Labour Party was unpatriotic'.[26]

On June 27, the NCL had appointed Dalton, Walter Citrine and Herbert Morrison 'to consult with the Prime Minister on various matters of national importance',[27] though nothing came of Chamberlain's subsequent offer to include some leading members of the Party in his administration. The September 2 meeting of the NEC and the executive committee of the PLP unanimously accepted a motion 'That the Party should not accept invitations to join the Government'.[28] This decision has an almost contemptuous ring to it – as if the leadership had instinctively realized the increase in the Party's political status with the advent of war. Labour's attitude to the government was neatly summarized by Dalton as being one of 'cold, critical, patriotic detachment'.[29] During September an electoral though not a parliamentary truce was negotiated, as was done in the 1914–18 war; later, Attlee explained that the consideration of having an alternative government available was an important factor in this decision.[30] At the time, Dalton noted that the 'so-called political truce was subject to termination at any time at our discretion'.[31] Attlee, in January 1940, had occasion to chide the Party's Secretary, James Middleton, for his assumption that under no circumstances would there be an appeal to the electorate until after the war. To assume that, Attlee declared, 'would be . . . a dangerous thing'.[32]

Viewed from outside at the beginning of the war, however, Labour still looked very much like a minority party, and a weak minority at that. At the 1935 general election Labour had obtained only 154 parliamentary seats to the Conservative's 432. In February 1939, a Gallup Poll indicated that for every 44 voters who supported the opposition parties, some 50 still preferred the government. By September 1939, Labour had only slightly improved on its parliamentary representation, gaining a mere 11 seats from the Conservatives. Such a situation tended to make the leadership cautious, at least in its public utterances. At the same time, the Party's extremists were emboldened, for the entire emotional and ideological legacy of the inter-war years did not evaporate overnight. It was one thing for the Party as a whole to demand an ultimatum, quite another for it collectively to contemplate the actual waging of war. The essence of Labour's relief at the state of affairs in September 1939 is not to be found in any considerable opinion that war was the answer to the problem of *Germany*: rather the emphasis must be placed on the Party's almost united opinion that a declaration of war was the sole remaining possibility of resolving the problem of *Nazism*.

For the Labour Party, the Second World War was in origin Hitler's War,[33] a war into which it had been forced. The point on which all members agreed at the outset was that they were 'fighting' Nazism, not the German people.

Labour had appealed to the German people before the outbreak of war. 'We are your friends,' a statement issued by the NCL on June 30 declared:

> ... no one wishes to make war on Germany ... War in fact threatens you not from outside but from inside your own country, and the responsibility for that threat belongs to Herr Hitler and his Government.[34]

The statement urged the Germans 'to do whatever you can to make it known to your Government that you want Peace and not War', but it also added that, 'what we cannot submit to is that we should be black-mailed and threatened by egotistic Dictators'. Dalton, who attended the NCL meeting, noted that it was decided to put this view 'over the air from all possible directions ...'. The statement was also to be circulated in Germany through underground channels.[35] Much the same note was struck by the NCL's *Message to the German People* on August 25. Warning that war was very near, the *Message* stated that nevertheless there was still time 'to save Peace and build a new Europe which would be based neither on Versailles nor Brest-Litovsk'. 'Remember,' the *Message* argued, 'it is you and we who will pay for the War.' Labour believed that it was not the German people who wanted war; it was 'a small handful of your rulers'.[36] The strength of this view within the Party is attested to by the efforts of Dalton (who almost certainly did not subscribe to it), and Citrine, to have the *Message* broadcast. These efforts, after a determined struggle, eventually met with success.[37]

In the Commons, on the day the ultimatum expired, Greenwood stressed that it was 'Nazism' which 'must be finally overthrown'.[38] Similarly, the TUC at its annual conference put the blame for the war on Germany's rulers who would be held 'personally responsible'. The general council's declaration also appealed to 'those of the German people who are conscious of the dreadful crime their ruler [had] committed in forcing [the] war' and in particular to the German workers 'who, we believe, have never lost their sense of comradeship and loyalty to the principles upon which the cause of the organized workers is founded'. Citrine emphasized that they had 'no general quarrel with the German people as such'.[39] The Left wing entirely agreed; Sir Stafford Cripps noted that 'Our enemy is Hitler and the Nazi régime, and not the German people . . .'[40] The *New Statesman*'s leading article immediately following the declaration of war praised the 'dropping [of] leaflets instead of bombs on the towns of Germany' as a 'right and imaginative stroke, of good augury for the future . . . to enlighten the German people about the behaviour of their rulers is the most important of all the tasks before us'.[41]

This distinction between the Nazis and the German people remained a cardinal tenet of all official Labour pronouncements on the war until 1943, and was never relinquished by the Left wing. Internationally, the distinction's significance was its implication that 'the other Germany' was entitled to play a full part in European affairs. During the 'phoney' or 'bore' war period the immediate corollary was the hope that the war might not have to be seriously 'fought' at all; a revolution inside Germany would largely suffice, so far as the blood-letting was concerned. This feeling readily allied itself to the complete lack of confidence in the competence of the Chamberlain government, quite apart from the deep personal antagonism which separated the parties, or the widespread Labour suspicions of Chamberlain's motives. In the event, all these factors were largely resolved for the Party by the actions of Hitler himself. But, at the beginning of the war, the feeling of relief was succeeded by certain Labour doubts as to the form the war might take, the aims for which it would be fought and its possible outcome.

Second Thoughts on the Left

THE sole indication given by the Labour leadership as to the form an actual war might take was contained in the *Message to the German People*.[1] Pointing out that Germany needed raw materials and food-stuffs, the *Message* had stated that she would find it very difficult to obtain these because of a 'rigorous naval blockade'. But there was no offensive on the part of Britain or France, just as there was no imme-diate aerial bombardment by the Germans. From a British point of view, the early nature of the war was somewhat analogous to the siren which Morrison had heard on September 3, a false alarm.

Such was not the case, of course, with Poland, whose rapid defeat was followed by an equally rapid occupation, by both Germany and Russia. Hitler and Stalin jointly declared on September 29 that as Poland was now partitioned between their respective states all respon-sibility for the continuation of the war rested with the Western Powers. On October 6, Hitler proposed a peace conference. The Anglo-French ultimatum, clearly, had failed to save Poland and in these circumstances many people in Britain, not only on the Left, began to have second thoughts. For them, the war's early developments were neither boring nor 'phoney' – a term invented later. Instead, and for a variety of reasons, they could be construed as offering a possible last chance by which the 'supreme barbarity of war' (in Kingsley Martin's phrase) might yet be avoided.

Martin, on September 25, admitted to Oliver Harvey, private secretary to Lord Halifax, that there was a great deal of pacifism among his readers.[2] His journal, the *New Statesman*, reflected the uneasiness about the war situation that this attitude generated. Though carefully dissociating itself from the idea of making peace on any or no terms – as implied in an article by Bernard Shaw in the October 7 issue – the paper argued that it would be most unwise to reject outright an ex-pected offer which had not yet been received and whose nature was still unknown. The strong point of Shaw's article, the paper considered, was that the war had become a different war since the Soviet Union had entered Poland. No further commitments should be made until much more was known about the Soviet Union's policy and intentions, though the object, whatever the method, remained that of freeing Europe and Germany of Nazism. The best and possibly the only chance was to talk with the German people rather than the Nazis . . . For all of which the paper received, and felt obliged to publish, a stinging rebuke from the celebrated economist J. M. Keynes: 'The intelligentsia of the Left were the loudest in demanding that the Nazi aggression should be resisted at all costs,' he wrote. 'When it comes to a show-down, scarce four weeks have passed before they remember that they are pacifists . . . leaving the defence of civilization to Colonel Blimp and the Old School Tie, for whom Three Cheers.'[3]

There were, nevertheless, other Left-wing opinions – notably those to be found in the columns of *Tribune*, the literary stronghold of the expelled Labour rebels Bevan and Cripps. Like its more intellectual companion on the Left, *Tribune* had had no hesitation, at first, in urging its readers to support the war. Articles by Bevan, Cripps and Konni Zilliacus, a prominent *Tribune* commentator on international affairs, also stressed other considerations. Bevan and Cripps warned that the conflict could develop into something other than an anti-Fascist war: Zilliacus described the situation as 'a class war as well as an international war': and he confidently predicted that it would end with revolutions in the Fascist countries.[4] This last was a classic Left-wing view which had been widely held prior to the First World War. Then, it was hoped, an international general strike would quickly put an end to hostilities and, perhaps, much else as well. Now, it was believed, the war would principally take the form of an uprising inside Germany. The non-realization of this belief was perhaps the greatest single ideological blow to the Left during the entire conflict.[5]

Bevan and Cripps, however, realized and indicated in the first wartime edition of *Tribune* that there was a possibility of the war lasting a good deal longer than many people thought, and that a German revolt was less likely the longer the war did last. Their immediate reaction was to stress the need, even more urgent than before, for a change in the British government. This was necessary both to prevent the conflict from degenerating into a war of rival imperialisms and also for the working class of the world to seize the opportunity of war 'to do something effective to save themselves from fresh tragedies and suffering'. Above all, the question of the peace terms which would be negotiated or imposed had to be kept in mind. Another peace like Versailles would only lead to another war.[6] But shortly afterwards Bevan and Cripps diverged in their attitudes.

Of the two Labour rebels, Cripps was by far the most influential at this time, and it was he who took the initiative in a re-assessment of the situation. Coming from a solidly established English family Cripps, before engaging in political activity, had won an enviable reputation as a legal advocate. Subsequently, he had adopted extreme Left-wing views while retaining his Anglican religious faith. In the late 1930s Cripps had been the prime mover in a series of attempts to promote a common political front, with Communists and others, against Fascism and capitalism. For this he had, in May 1939, been expelled from the Labour Party – as had Bevan and others. But whereas Bevan was re-admitted before the end of the year, Cripps was not. Bevan did not budge from his position of no compromise with Nazism; Cripps did, albeit in a qualified way.

In the *Tribune* of September 15, Cripps elaborated his original theme. Although there could be no compromise with 'Nazism or with the present rulers of Germany', this did not preclude negotiations with the German people – 'as soon as they can tell us authoritatively through reliable sources that they have asserted themselves as the free and honourable people we know them to be'. Territorial questions had to be considered less important than economic ones in the future. This meant that only the working class in both Britain and Germany could be trusted to make the peace, because they had no vested interests. He hoped they would have the aid of the USSR when the time came for practical steps in peace-making. *Tribune*'s foreign affairs correspondent supported this by arguing that the war could be shortened if friendly contact with the USSR were to be restored. He attacked the popular Labour daily newspaper, the *Daily Herald*, and Citrine, of the TUC, for their anti-Russian position. Zilliacus strongly agreed with the need to establish an understanding with the Soviet Union. He called for the Labour Party to make a more precise statement of peace aims and, in the meantime, offered his own suggestions. These included no secret treaties and no dictated peace, but also no cessation of fighting until the German people had overthrown the Nazi régime. He stressed the necessity for a British peace offer before the war had intensified to a point where it would be difficult to persuade people to distinguish between Germans and Nazis. Not to be outdone by other Left-wingers, Cripps – after the occupation of Poland – underlined his own position. 'Why blame Russia?' he challenged. The Russians had been driven to do what they did for their own security and because neither the British, French nor Poles were capable of protecting Poland from the Nazis.[7]

But the Labour leadership had blamed Russia. Greenwood, in the *Daily Herald*, stated bluntly that the invasion of Poland by the USSR had been done on grounds which could not be justified.[8] Attlee was more adroit – he contented himself with saying that 'Poland will rise again'.[9] Even so, it is clear that the leadership in general resisted with difficulty the temptation to take an outright anti-Russian line – an attitude which has to be seen in terms of the legacy from the 1930s. In the first place, Russia symbolized an anti-Labour totalitarian communism. Secondly, with one notable exception, the leadership did not look favourably then or later on the prospect of any major extension of Soviet power in Europe. Neither was this attitude confined to the leadership. A back-bench Welsh miner MP, David Grenfell, declared in the Commons that there would only be talk of peace if Europe went back at least as far as the *status quo ante*-Munich.[10]

Cripps now shifted his ground. He had become convinced that the chances of a German revolt had been over-estimated. If continued, the war would probably last much more than three years and the British Empire and British capitalism would never stand the strain, even if they managed to survive as conquerors.[11] There was no point, he told the Commons on October 12, in continuing a war merely because one's opponents could not be trusted.[12] Cripps made it clear in *Tribune* that he was prepared to negotiate with Hitler if Russia could be induced to guarantee an agreement. The alternative was the worst war that civilization had ever known.[13] Other *Tribune* writers remained adamant that no peace was worth having which did not lead to the downfall of the Nazi régime. Criticism of the Labour leadership redoubled, perhaps in order to conceal the divergence of opinion on the Left. It was condemned for not stating its peace aims; it was accused of not being able to make up its mind, of failing to relate ends to means and, in particular, of not accepting the necessity of co-operation with the USSR.

But though there was some truth in these charges, the leadership's dilemma was seriously underestimated. There was not merely the emerging analysis of the Left wing to be considered; Labour had also to reckon with the government. What distinguished Labour here was not so much hesitation in regard to Russia as a rigid posture in regard to Nazi Germany. Chamberlain still considered himself free to negotiate with Hitler; the reason for the British government's refusal to state its war aims in more specific terms was – as the Canadian government was informed – 'if Herr Hitler wants to negotiate, we have given him the chance to do so'.[14] This option was 'ideologically' out of the question for Labour's leaders.

One of these had made up his mind about the war, though not from a premise that either the Left or many of the hierarchy would have accepted at this time. In outward appearance Hugh Dalton presented almost a caricature of the dyed-in-the-wool Tory background from which he had sprung. Tall in stature, aggressive in manner, bombastic in voice, Dalton was a supremely self-confident if singularly unusual Labour leader, both in his character and in his views. He desired from the very beginning of the war to see and, if possible, to bring about a drastic and permanent reduction in the actual and potential power of Germany. 'Others believe,' he confided to his diary,

> that there is always a 'good old Germany' just around the corner. They hope for just a small change, a Government of Generals, or even a Monarchist restoration, and then all danger will be passed. This, too, is an illusion. There is no 'good old Germany' just around the corner.

He was fully aware of the implications but, in a very different way from the Left, took a sanguine view of Russia. Though he considered that the Russians had 'long since passed away from Communism . . . had become first Nationalists and now Imperialists', this did not trouble him:

> Even supposing that the Red Army overran, or got control of, all Poland, part of Germany and the Czech and Slovak lands, [a remarkable forecast in October 1939!] so that there emerged a Polish, a German, a Slovak and a Czech Soviet Socialist Republic, I did not feel that this would be a stable constellation, or that it could be run from Moscow. But I would greatly prefer a development of that kind to the continuance of Hitler Germany with its Protectorates.

29

His reason for paying such a price, if it were necessary, was his conviction that 'Until the leaders of the Nazi Party have been physically exterminated, and until the German military class has been broken, there can be no hope of steady peace in Europe.' However, it was 'much too soon to say this, or anything like this in public . . . or we shall simply drive together these two very dangerous classes'.

During the autumn of 1939 then, Dalton set about influencing people in private. He suggested both to R. A. Butler, then Under-Secretary of State at the Foreign Office, and to Polish Embassy officials that, after the war, Poland should be prepared to be content with the Curzon Line* as its Eastern frontier, while being compensated with East Prussia. With the Poles he agreed that the transfer of populations, 'now that Hitler has taken it up officially', should be carried much further in any post-war settlement; but he was much less forthcoming to the French, who had also spoken to him of future German dismemberment. He described the suggestion of a separated Rhineland being subsequently assimilated to France as 'short-sighted and stupid'.[15] But Dalton's major sphere of influence, naturally, was to be within the Labour Party itself.

Before considering the leadership's official response to the war's first developments, one other Labour faction must be mentioned which in this context can neither be labelled Right nor Left wing. The pure pacifists had always been prepared to talk with the Nazis – or anyone else – if the subject was peace. By themselves they composed only a small minority of the PLP – about ten per cent – and their influence had been on the wane since 1935. The changed circumstances now lent, or appeared to lend, this group a new political potential. The unease among certain elements on the Left was also reflected outside Labour ranks,[16] notably by Lloyd George.[17] After a few weeks of the 'war', the old Liberal leader and former Prime Minister 'was becoming convinced of Allied inability to win'. But Lloyd George, though not lacking useful friends elsewhere, had no significant parliamentary strength. One Labour MP, himself a non-pacifist, decided to use the pacifists in an approach to Lloyd George: R. R. Stokes – 'a Catholic, an arms manufacturer, land-taxer, and future minister in the 1945–51 Labour government' – formed the Peace Aims Group, whose mem-

---

* *ie*, the line proposed to the Soviet government as the basis for a settlement by Lord Curzon, the British Secretary of State for Foreign Affairs, in July 1920.

bership would appear to have fluctuated from a possible maximum of twenty-five MPs, plus a few peers, downwards. Declaring that he had already fought the Germans for three years to no avail in the First World War, Stokes attempted to involve his creation in a series of 'compromise peace' moves from 1939 to 1942.[18]

The idea of an approach to Lloyd George gathered momentum after the latter's famous speech in the Commons on October 3. Lloyd George told the House that if a peace proposal were received from a neutral power (and he included Russia and Italy as neutrals), it should not be dismissed out of hand. Instead a secret session of Parliament should be called.[19] Kingsley Martin, who was in touch with the old war leader, agreed. The *New Statesman* announced on October 28 that 'The only statesman, and he unfortunately is an elder statesman, who frankly faces the facts in Britain today is Mr Lloyd George'. Quite apart from his own pacifist tendencies, Martin took the view that – as he put it to Harold Nicolson – 'we cannot possibly beat both Russia and Germany'. Nicolson, then a National Labour MP, was worried that a peace-at-any-price school might spread rapidly across the whole political spectrum.[20] The essence of Stokes's personal position is to be found in a memorandum of his which reached Lloyd George in October 1939. 'Are we really content,' Stokes asked, 'to bring our own civilization to ruin in order that the Hammer and Sickle shall fly from the North Sea to the Pacific?'[21] But while the predominant section in the Labour Party was as anti-Communist as it was anti-Nazi, Stokes appears to have been virtually alone in according the former priority over the latter.

Meanwhile, the International Affairs sub-committee of the NEC had spent most of September considering various proposals regarding the basis of a peace settlement. The committee concluded that the movement's general policy should be clarified and this view was brought before the NCL on September 26. Here, the Party representatives discovered that because of the declaration adopted by the TUC at its annual conference held at Bridlington, on the initiative of the general council, the industrial members of the NCL were unwilling to issue any further statements on the subject for the present. All that the NEC of the Party could do on September 27 was to accept a resolution moved by Dalton that the International Affairs sub-committee should continue its examination and report back, and that Harold Laski be added to the committee. Morrison and Laski then moved that it be understood that, before any statement of war aims be issued, exploratory consultations with representatives of the French Socialist Party would be essential and, at a later stage, so would discussion with the full executive committee of the Labour and Socialist International. This was accepted.[22]

In the Commons, therefore, Attlee (now restored to health) was obliged to limit himself to a simple reiteration of the Party's anti-Hitler stand. 'We shall require deeds, and not merely words before we get any substantial basis for peace . . .,' he stated on October 3.[23] After Chamberlain's rejection of Hitler's peace offer, on October 12, in words almost identical to those used previously by Attlee, the Labour leader was more explicit. The so-called peace proposals, he declared, had been made by 'a man whose word is utterly worthless and [they] offer nothing but vague future promises'; they had been made after brutal and unprovoked aggression and they were based on the acceptance of that aggression as a *fait accompli*; there was no indication of any change of heart or mind on which hopes for the future could be founded. Yet Attlee was careful to emphasize that Labour sought no Carthaginian peace; he called for a 'more closely co-ordinated Europe' in the future, in which the rights of all nations, including the small ones, would be respected. The choice before the German people was:

> . . . not of being defeated in war and disappearing as effective members of the European comity of nations. They have the choice of stopping this war, they have the choice of contributing to a great Europe . . . But until we get people on whose word we can rely we must with resolution pursue this struggle . . .[24]

At the next meeting of the NEC, on October 25, the question of a statement of war aims was raised again. It was reported that requests for such a statement had been made by some forty affiliated constituency parties. The International Affairs sub-committee had in fact prepared and circulated a document,[25] but on October 12 the representatives of the general council (of the TUC) had again indicated that they were not prepared to consider the issue of any statement at that time. They had agreed, however, that pronouncements already made by the leader, deputy leader, the NEC and the TUC at Bridlington should be examined regarding the preparation of a draft document for further discussion. This was ready in time for the NCL meeting on

October 20, but, without even discussing its terms, the meeting had decided that no official statement should be issued by the NCL or brought to the attention of the three national committees for immediate use. Instead, it was suggested that the Party's position might be met for the time being by Mr Attlee making a public declaration. After lengthy discussion, the NEC agreed. The document originally prepared and circulated by the International Affairs sub-committee was read and its general terms approved for Attlee's guidance.[26]

Such was the internal Party background to Attlee's speech on November 8, which was later published by the Party as *Labour's Peace Aims*.[27] The title, though an explicit challenge to Stokes's Group, is nevertheless indicative of the leadership's concern for Party unity. The statement contained nothing that was new, and must be regarded largely as an effort to rally Party opinion behind the leadership. It included an appeal by Attlee to the rank and file to educate itself in the principles of Labour's international outlook in the light of the situation created by the war. There was still no indication that such a war might have to be fought and Henry Pelling has commented that the trade unions 'shared the mood of the country in their unwillingness to accept the logical consequences of their verbal commitment to the war effort'.[28] Yet there was also no indication that the war might not have to be fought. The main points of the statement may be summarized as follows:

(1) No dictated peace, revenge or punishment. In particular, there was 'no desire to humiliate, to crush, or to divide the German nation'. But restitution would have to be made to victims of aggression.
(2) National self-determination.
(3) Abandonment of aggression and armed forces.
(4) Recognition of religious, racial and national minorities.
(5) Creation of an international authority, and the reiteration of the idea that 'Europe must federate or perish'.
(6) Abandonment of imperialism, and equal access by all nations to markets and raw materials.

Within the framework of the Labour debate which had preceded it and also that which accompanied it in November, the statement is noteworthy in three respects. First, it is abundantly clear that the Labour hierarchy countenanced no dealing of any kind with the Nazis – a note sounded again later that same month in a broadcast by Morrison. He explained that they were fighting for the 'Rights of Man'.[29] Second, there is the studied moderation in regard to the question of Germany's frontiers. And, third, there is the absence of any reference to 'Socialism' – a point which Attlee rather casually corrected on November 28 when he told the Commons, 'The fact is that if you want to win this war you will have to have a great deal of practical Socialism.'[30]

Attlee's statement, couched as it was in traditional Socialist terms, did not succeed in stilling the intellectual ferment on the Left. The month of November brought forth an autumnal flurry of interpretations and comments, of which the two most noteworthy were by Harold Laski and G. D. H. Cole. Laski, the well-known political scientist and the most influential Left-wing theoretician on the NEC, published a pamphlet of his own, though under the auspices of the Party.[31] He urged that Labour must press for a peace which would involve not merely the defeat of Hitlerism, but also the removal of the causes of such forms of fascism. This pamphlet marked the formal beginning of a theme which he was to pursue from his position within the innermost circles of the Party throughout the war. G. D. H. Cole was another leading Left-wing academic and a prolific writer. From a more independent position, in one of the most widely-read pronouncements at this time,[32] he elaborated the view which had previously brought down Keynes's strictures. Cole roundly condemned the Labour Party – for appearing to rest content with rallying behind the government in the name of national unity against Hitler. He also condemned Hitler and Stalin. Yet what was uppermost in Cole's mind was his abhorrence of the war being fought. Like Cripps, he came down in favour of negotiations with Hitler's Germany if conducted openly and with the participation of the neutrals.

By November, also, the pacifists had re-grouped their forces. Every possible influence was exerted, both in private and in public. The burden of their effort may be gathered from a letter signed by some twenty MPs of the Peace Aims Group which, no doubt because of the Group's size, was published in the *Daily Herald*. The letter urged that a negotiated peace be secured as early as possible and that such a peace had to include some surrender of national sovereignty in a new European system, a standstill in armaments, economic internationalism, and the widest possible extension of self-government in the world. There was no mention of Hitler.[33]

34

It was *Tribune*'s readers, however, who were most directly confronted with evidence of division on the Left. The emphasis which all the paper's contributors placed upon the necessity of changing the government served mainly to underline this division. One editorial, on November 10, went so far as to suggest that it was academic to talk under the existing circumstances of any peace aims that a socialist should accept, since it was impossible to get the government to adopt such aims or to carry them out. The Labour rebel who concentrated most on this theme was the articulate and passionate Welsh MP, Aneurin Bevan. His silence on the 'academic' but nevertheless fervent discussion of war aims during November is instructive. It lends credence to his biographer's contention that he 'never doubted the war would have to be fought'[34] – and serves to distinguish him from many others on the Left. Bevan devoted his literary energy during the month to showing how 'the workers' could make their presence felt.

He had two main suggestions. The first was the necessity of keeping open the channel of parliamentary debate. What worried Bevan was that, though the government had shown some evidence during the first two months of the war of willingness to accommodate the wishes of the opposition regarding debates, etc., this might not last. Once it became clear that Labour supported the war for one purpose, and the government for another, then the moral support for burdens on the home front would be drained away and domestic strife would begin. In Bevan's opinion, it was this which had led 'certain shrewd persons' to resist the demand for the re-formulation of Labour's peace aims. Now that these had been formulated the next step would be their translation from an academic essay into a working plan of immediate struggle – against the government. Bevan's second suggestion was that such action should come from the industrial wing of the movement. Towards the end of the month he went one step further and called for the ending of the political truce. He realized that a general election would be found impossible; what he favoured was complete freedom for individual MPs and the exclusion of by-elections from the truce.

'Academic' or not, the discussion of the broader issue continued unabated elsewhere in *Tribune*. Sir Charles Trevelyan was among a number of former Liberal MPs who, mainly as a result of their opposition to the First World War, had joined the Labour Party. Along with Cripps and Bevan he, too, had been expelled from the Party in May 1939. His thesis was the need for world security, an international federation of nations, not dictation to Germany. He had little confidence that either the Chamberlain government or the Labour opposition, as then led, could achieve these aims.[35] Cole indicated that his views had changed. No one could now prophesy what would happen, but he still ventured to disagree with Trevelyan's aim of a world-wide federalism on the grounds of its impossibility. Instead, he argued that the main aim should be 'a federalism based primarily upon Western Europe'. 'Vigilans',[36] the *Tribune* writer who succeeded Zilliacus, could see no alternative to a policy of support for the war and opposition to Chamberlain. He condemned the proposal that Britain should enter a peace conference while Hitler was still in power and in possession of Czechoslovakia and Poland. But while agreeing with the Labour leadership that there should be no dictated peace, no revenge and that all nations should be parties to the peace, he interpreted this to mean 'the repudiation of the whole idea of military victory . . .'.[37] *Tribune*'s editor recorded that a very large number of letters had been received criticizing 'Vigilans', and printed a selection of them. All were against the war because it was imperialist, which was the current Communist Party line.

The Left, then, was thoroughly divided. To all intents and purposes the fellow-travellers, on the one hand, and Stokes plus the Peace Aimers on the other, were reduced to treading the same path, which was not far removed from that of Chamberlain. The 'intellectuals', overcome by their genuine abhorrence of war and yet equally opposed to the Nazi régime, could not rid themselves of the hope, or rather illusion, that a social revolution in Europe could be brought about without the 'locomotive of war'. They, perforce, had to fall back on the assertion that Russia was the key to the whole situation, which was simply to resurrect the Labour policy of the 1930s.

Such a policy had not stemmed from any sympathy for Stalinist Russia. In addition, the Nazi-Soviet Pact had made a considerable impact upon the Labour leadership (apart from Dalton) – however much the responsibility for bringing it about could be attributed to Chamberlain. This was particularly true of the industrial wing, with its long memories of communist tactics in the trade unions. The Russian attack on Finland was to present the leadership with a further opportunity of consolidating its ideological grip on the Party. Given the confusion on the Left, and the ineffectiveness of pacifist opposition, it was an opportunity not to be missed in the months that followed.

CHAPTER III

Resolution by the Leadership

THERE can be little doubt that the Russian attack on Finland on November 30, 1939 was almost as welcome to Labour's leaders for domestic political reasons as it was repugnant to them on international grounds. Except for Attlee, who said nothing, the most moderate public comment on the part of the official leadership came from Dalton: 'an act of aggression had been committed by a great power against a small and democratic country', he told the Commons the same day, 'and in our view such action is indefensible'.[1] Thereafter the leadership exploded. 'The Union of Soviet Socialist Republics is dead. Stalin's new imperialist Russia takes its place,' editorialized the *Daily Herald* on December 1. Three days later an article by Greenwood pronounced that there was 'No Excuse For Russia'; and, on December 5, the *Herald*'s diplomatic correspondent described Stalin as a modern Genghis Khan. A statement by the NCL spoke of the Council's 'profound horror and indignation'. British Labour, it declared, utterly repudiated the claim of the Soviet government to be 'the interpreter of Socialist principles . . . Leader of the World's Working-Class Movement . . . custodian of International Peace . . .'. Furthermore, the statement called upon 'the free nations of the world' to give every practicable aid to the Finnish nation.[2]

The action taken by Labour in support of this polemic was another matter. In response to an appeal from the Finnish Labour Party and Trade Union general council for a leading Party representative to study the situation, the NCL unanimously agreed to send a team of three representatives.[3] But Dalton, who was Attlee's first choice, declined to go.[4] The sole result of the visit was the launching, by the Party and the TUC, of a special appeal in connection with the Aid to Finland Fund which the Party had established. A meeting of a Labour Party delegation[5] with leaders of the French Socialist Party (SFIO) in Paris, on February 22, 1940, to consider the general war situation did produce a joint resolution which included a reference to Stalin as 'Hitler's accomplice'. But the terms of this resolution owed much to the 'depressing' impression made on the Labour delegation by their 'French Comrades'.[6] Two days afterwards, while in Brussels for a meeting of the Labour and Socialist International, Dalton had to restrain the French Socialist leader, Léon Blum, who 'was for helping the Finns to the utmost at all costs, even though this led to war with Russia. I said I had no mandate for that.'[7]

What Angus Calder has called the 'hysteria in political circles'[8] at this time, so far as official Labour was concerned, largely followed the lines of the internal Party strife of the previous decade. An article by Attlee in the *Daily Herald* on February 21, 1940 was directed against the British Communist Party. The expulsion of D. N. Pritt, a member of the NEC, was a further warning to fellow-travellers.[9] By April 2, 1940, the *Daily Herald* pointedly editorialized that, 'In wartime a wise nation does not look for extra enemies. We are fighting Hitler.'

It was the Left who were most affected emotionally by the Russian action, in spite of a spirited defence attempt by Cripps and others. Only Bevan seems to have been completely unmoved. Cripps urged his *Tribune* readers on December 1, 1939, to 'Put Yourselves in Russia's Place'. He argued that Russia had been forced to adopt her present policy because her previous one had depended upon the co-operation of Britain and France. Bevan, in the same issue, merely advised the PLP to seize the opportunity presented by the war to make gains upon the domestic front. These gains could be made whether the war was imperialist or anti-fascist.

More Communist Party-type letters appeared in this issue of *Tribune* attacking 'Vigilans', but so too did an anonymous defender of the war policy. The latter poured scorn on the 'naive' assumption that the war was imperialist on the 1914–18 model. Chamberlain's motives were not those of Labour, of course, but wars were neither begun nor determined by the personal motives of statesmen. In any case, it was quite certain that neither Chamberlain nor British capitalism desired the war, especially against Nazi Germany. They were too well aware that it might release social forces far more dangerous to them than the 'unfair' methods of Nazi competition. Hitlerism was not primarily concerned with capitalist economics. The Nazi régime aimed at nothing less than the military occupation and the subjugation, physical and moral, of every state and nation not powerful enough to defend

itself. This letter was very close to official Labour's 'ideological' interpretation of the war.

Tribune's Board and 'Vigilans' issued a joint statement on the subject
of Russia and Finland on December 8, deploring the Russian attack
and condemning it as a blunder. At the same time, it warned its readers,
'comrades in the Labour Movement', not to allow themselves to be
used in an orgy of Red-baiting. It was not because she was an aggressor
that Russia was being 'attacked in certain quarters', but because she
was Socialist. *Tribune* would oppose any war against the Soviet Union,
and Bevan subsequently denounced the despatch of British arms to
Finland. Yet in so far as these reactions were directed against the Labour
hierarchy, rather than the Chamberlain government, they reflected
ideological weakness, if not disingenuousness.

Early in 1940 *Tribune* was obliged to record its partial agreement
with the Labour leadership's position. The most striking fact in the
situation, the paper considered, was that of military deadlock or stalemate. There was little or no chance that the war would turn in Britain's
favour if it were prolonged; it was far more probable that the Soviet
Union would come in increasingly on the side of Germany than that
the benevolent neutrality of the United States would turn into an
effective partnership with the Allies. On the other hand, the paper
could find very little promise in the idea of a negotiated peace either.
In these circumstances the only option for the Left was to urge that the
Allied governments should adopt a programme such as Labour's Peace
Aims. As the war dragged on, and the German people despaired of
either peace or victory, a standing offer of a world settlement based on
these Aims would operate more and more powerfully to disintegrate
the moral cohesion of the Nazi régime. The article significantly concluded that 'the former policy of the Left – building up a peace bloc
composed of the USSR and the Western democracies to resist Fascist
aggression – now lacks almost all basis in reality'. There only remained
the necessity of opposing war with the Soviet Union for as long as
possible and the need to insist on negotiations with Russia. The paper
now agreed formally with 'Vigilans', who had suggested it earlier, that
'The starting point for Left foreign policy today is Anglo-French
relations'.[10] A week later the directors of *Tribune*, Bevan and G. R.
Strauss, both now re-admitted to the Labour Party, announced the
departure of the paper's editor, H. J. Hartshorn.

In fact, while the Russo-Finnish War and the Nazi-Soviet entente continued, the Left plumbed the depths of gloom and despair. An unsigned editorial in the *New Statesman* described what it called 'the heart of the problem'. The struggle was now not only between the land powers and the Western sea powers, it was also

> between the totalitarian brave new world and the old world of Western Europe. The Totalitarians, whether Nazi or Communist, are fighting to conquer not merely the territories of the west, but the spirit of man: their wars are revolutionary wars and at the same time wars of two secular religions upon a doubting, insecure and unhappy world.[11]

The few months prior to the Party's annual conference in May 1940 were equally grim for *Tribune*'s writers and readers. True, Victor Gollancz, the Left-wing publisher, was heartened by the end of the Russo-Finnish War, while Bevan relentlessly pursued his attacks on the Chamberlain government. The paper continued to urge caution in respect of Russia, and took particular exception to the Labour and French Socialist Parties joint resolution passed in Paris; *Tribune* emphasized that a non-aggression pact did not mean that Russia had yet taken sides. The same editorial also suggested that 'American mediation may become literally of vital importance'. But nothing could shake the overall gloom. Russia had behaved, wrote Raymond Postgate, the new editor, 'as we hoped no Socialist State ever would behave'; and there was now 'no possibility of a mass movement against the Nazis in Germany'. Gollancz warned his former close associates of Popular Front days, who had been crying 'Stop the Imperialist War', that if they gambled on international working-class action stopping the war, and it did not succeed, the result would be the immediate destruction of the working-class movement, as had happened in Germany and Poland. There was no point, he reminded them, in repeating the slogans of the 1914–18 war as that had occurred before the rise of 'fascism and the totalitarian technique'. Postgate neatly summarized the situation of –

> ... very many stalwart members of the Labour Movement; ... They cannot accept the pacifist pretence that all would be well if Hitler's terms were accepted. They will never trust the Communist Party again. They think the PLP has no lead to offer them. They see the Government which lost the peace rapidly engaged in losing the war ...[12]

The pacifist as well as Left-wing position was defeated in 1940. In January, James Middleton and G. R. Shepherd, the secretary and national agent respectively of the Party, wrote to constituency organizations that no attacks were to be made on official Party candidates or Policy by pacifist members. No opposition could be overlooked; pacifists would be treated with the utmost understanding – provided (essentially) that they kept their views to themselves.[13] Lansbury's death, on May 7, 1940, symbolized the end of an era in Labour politics and it is highly doubtful in any case whether the numerical strength of the pacifists in the PLP fairly reflected rank and file opinion. Those inclined to ideas of a negotiated peace were fated to be voices crying in the wilderness or insignificant meeting places, letter-writers to politicians whose day had long since passed. Given the strength of Labour's detestation of the Nazi régime (which, ironically, was shared by the pacifists), the realization that Hitler enjoyed considerable support in Germany and, finally, the beginning of the German attack in the West, the compromise peace faction at no time appeared capable of swaying the Party.

Stokes looked elsewhere. In January, he managed to have an interview with von Papen, the German ambassador to Turkey. Notes of this talk were given to R. A. Butler at the Foreign Office and to Lloyd George,[14] but nothing came of it. Further meetings of the Peace Aims Group were held, and various deputations and communications were sent to the former Prime Minister as late as June and July. Stokes also continued to communicate with Lloyd George after the fall of France. Now his argument – and it was not far removed from that of the chiefs of staff – was that the only way in which Britain could conceivably defeat Germany militarily was by means of a blockade. Such a 'starvation defeat', he reasoned, would simply worsen the European situation. Even if they succeeded in bringing about the overthrow of Hitler by force, the result could well be a communist revolution. Thus Stokes and the British Communists opposed the war for exactly opposite reasons, though Stokes at least seemed to realize that his was a lost cause; he headed his letter, 'Impertinent Memorandum probably too late'.[15]

Meanwhile, the Labour hierarchy had continued to wrestle with the problem of an official pronouncement. A draft statement, 'Labour and the War', was accepted by the International Affairs sub-committee and the emergency executive committee of the Party[16] and, on

January 25, 1940, sent out to all members of the NEC for comment. In view of the nature of some of the replies a special meeting of the NEC was called on February 6 to reconsider the draft. Here, the section on Finland was changed somewhat. As well, Laski and Ellen Wilkinson, MP for Gateshead, tried to get something included about India, but their motion was lost by 4 votes to 9.[17] Even then, Attlee was still unhappy and would not vote for the document. James Griffiths, a middle-of-the-road Party loyalist, would have made trouble had he been at the meeting, Dalton thought, and the extreme Left-winger Pritt voted against it.[18] Hence the meeting set up a further committee, of Morrison, Dalton and Laski, empowering them to review the statement as a whole, re-draft it where necessary, and publish it.

What Attlee objected to was the phrase that, in the future, in resistance to any potential German aggression, the British and French 'must not be merely allies for a season, but brothers for all time'. According to Dalton again, Attlee thought that there was too much about Germany and France in the document.[19] Dalton had a very low opinion of Attlee at the beginning of the war, privately referring to him as 'The Rabbit' as an expression of his conviction that Attlee 'at no time . . . is big enough or strong enough to carry the burden',[20] – of leadership. But, quite apart from his personal opinion, Attlee had what he conceived to be the interests of party unity strongly in mind. Later that month, at the joint British and French party meeting in Paris, Attlee was prepared to subscribe to a communiqué stating that the two Parties were resolved 'from now onwards to work for an ever closer union of the French and British peoples because they are convinced that this unity which is indispensable for victory today will form the essential basis of the new order'.[21]

The final version of Labour's statement, under the new title 'Labour, the War and the Peace' was published on February 9.[22] It contained a new sub-section headed 'For Socialism and Freedom', instead of a previous paragraph 'Britain's Historic Task' – which almost certainly reflected Laski's influence. The overthrow of the 'Hitler system in Germany' was deemed 'essential to the achievement of Labour's programme of social justice, the maintenance and extension of democratic liberties and the building of a peaceful commonwealth of free peoples'. Emphasizing Labour's condemnation of the British government's clumsiness in its earlier relations with the Soviet Union, the statement insisted that this clumsiness could not excuse the Russian government's Pact with the Nazis, 'much less its unprovoked attack on Finland in shameless imitation of the Nazi technique in foreign policy. We should regard the extinction of the free Finnish democracy as an intolerable disaster for civilization.' It may be imagined that the words of this last sentence were very carefully chosen indeed.

So also was the pronouncement that:

> The French claim to security had to be reconciled with the German claim to Equality . . . [and that] any attempt to keep Germany an outcast after this war, or to deprive her of such security as her neighbours rightly claim for themselves, will fail. The most far-sighted and least dangerous policy is to seek to win the co-operation, as an equal partner, of a Germany governed by a political system whose needs and aims run parallel with ours.

This accorded with the demand that 'undertakings . . . be given to the German people that, in the general rearrangement after the war, the just and real interests of all people will be respected, including those of the German people'. The Labour Party was 'opposed to any attempt from outside to break up Germany', though a warning was given that while Hitler and his system prepared and started the war, he could not continue if the Germans ceased to support him. The Labour Party was also convinced that the Allies ought not to enter into peace negotiations, except with a German government which had not merely promised but had actually performed certain acts of restitution. These would include withdrawal from Poland and Czechoslovakia.

All this, however ('too much about Germany' notwithstanding), was a mere preamble to the important part of the statement. For the leadership now clarified its complete acceptance of the fact that the war would have to be fought. 'Victory is our immediate task,' the statement proclaimed: 'Victory for democracy must be achieved, either by arms or economic pressure, or – better still by a victory of the German people over the Hitler régime, resulting in the birth of a new Germany.' The last sentence of the statement was more precise: 'Victory must come to the *arms* of Britain, France and their Allies . . .'.

From February on, various Party leaders made it clear that they had no serious hopes of a German revolution substantially contributing to that victory. Herbert Morrison, in a long and carefully worked out speech on February 1, urged planning and national co-ordination on the government to facilitate the war effort. 'There was . . .,' he said, a tendency in the public mind in the early stages of the war – perhaps it was a little unwisely encouraged in official quarters – to assume that time was on our side without qualification, and that all we had to do was to sit back and hold tight and the war would be won.[23]

He set himself to undermine this assumption, referring to a recent speech by Bevin, in which the trade union leader had argued for a more closely co-ordinated authority in regard to transport, before any aerial bombardments began. Attlee actively supported Morrison,[24] and not only inside the Commons. Explaining to *Daily Herald* readers that they had to recognize 'that Hitler and his gangsters have – by the most brutal measures – established a very strong hold on the German people', Attlee boldly stated that Hitler's military and economic machine could not be defeated by half-measures. He made various suggestions for more efficient and vigorous organization, including a small war cabinet composed of ministers without departmental responsibilities.[25] Dalton, as he was later to admit, had badly misjudged his man.

Of greater significance to the more general question concerning Labour's foreign policy was the strictly empirical doctrine enunciated in 'Labour, the War and the Peace'. It was that of the lesser evil. 'The Labour Party,' it declared, 'unreservedly supports the Allied war of resistance to Nazi aggression because, though loathing war, it regards this war as a lesser evil than the slavery which finally would be the only alternative.' So much for the pacifist and compromise peace element. The doctrine clearly facilitated, also, the entry of Labour into the Coalition – from an 'ideological' standpoint, that is. It was endorsed notably by two very different members of the NEC in the course of the year. Laski, in his pamphlet 'Is This an Imperialist War?'[26] – which was addressed explicitly to the more 'ideologically-minded' faction – provocatively answered his own question in the affirmative. But then he added that Nazi imperialism differed qualitatively from British and French imperialism in that while the former was expanding, the latter was contracting. Therefore, 'The risk to Democracy is one that history compels Socialists to take in order to avoid the infinitely greater risk to it that would be involved in Hitler's victory.' Attlee, eschewing the political metaphysics of the professor and the 'history compels' approach, put it more simply and effectively. For him, it was a question of the very survival of the Labour movement. Moving an emergency resolution proposing that Labour should

44

join a coalition government at the Party's annual conference, Attlee remarked that, 'Whatever may be the conditions in the capitalist democracies, there is always that hope, there is always that opportunity [of preserving the Labour movement] . . . but where Nazism reigns, all hope has gone.'[27]

Before the conference began, Cole had come to agree with Laski, Ellen Wilkinson and others on the Left that the war would have to be fought and that Labour must play a vital part in winning it. They disagreed, however, as to how this might be achieved; Cole did not want Labour to join the government, Ellen Wilkinson wanted the complete equality of Labour in the government, and Laski wanted a fundamental change of government.[28] Raymond Postgate sounded a more positive note. He pointed out that the immense increase in the power of the working class was likely to continue and with it the industrial and political power of the movement. They must not therefore be afraid of responsibility, but must act with 'a double end in view – to win the war and in so doing to change society so that capitalism does not survive it'.[29]

Parliamentary events then took an unexpected course. The fiasco of the Norwegian campaign produced 'what Labour disgruntlement had not the power to enforce and what Tory independence had not the daring to demand'[30] – the downfall of Chamberlain. This was not achieved without considerable irony; Chamberlain was not actually defeated in the House, and might, indeed, have secured a larger majority had it not been for his own famous and fatuous intervention in the debate; the principal beneficiary turned out to be Churchill, the man most responsible for the Norwegian campaign; and Labour's own role in the episode owed more to opportunism than deliberate strategy. The story of the historic debate and its accompanying intrigues has been told so often that it needs no elaboration here; instead, three aspects of it may be singled out.

Firstly, there is the question of the Labour leadership's hesitation about bringing the issue to a vote; the announcement that a vote would be forced was made only on the second day of the debate. According to Morrison, 'neither Attlee nor almost any member of the Labour Party front bench committee had considered what to do . . .'[31] but this is not borne out by the Conservative MP, L. S. Amery. He states that Attlee had been approached by Clement Davies, the Liberal leader, on May 7, but had hesitated. The reason was tactical: 'it made it much easier for Conservatives to be influenced by the opening day's debate'.[32] It is also likely that Attlee wanted to avoid the risk of adding to the dismal succession of Chamberlain's massive parliamentary victories. But whether Attlee was then influenced by the trend of the debate (including the vigour of the speeches made by the rebel Conservatives), or by Morrison (who claims for himself the leading role in the decisive Labour front bench committee meeting[33]), or even whether Labour's hand was forced by the women MPs (as is argued by A. J. P. Taylor[34]) remains a moot point.

Secondly, there is the possibility that Labour would have preferred to serve under Halifax rather than Churchill. Attlee's retrospective comment was that he would have supported anyone who would have got on with the war.[35] Stafford Cripps had suggested Halifax as Prime Minister on May 6.[36] As it happened, the NEC was unanimously 'prepared to take its share of responsibility as a full member in a new Government, under a new Prime Minister, which would command the confidence of the nation'.[37] Churchill's subsequent offer that Labour should join a government formed by him was accepted, on Attlee's and Greenwood's recommendation, by 17 NEC votes to 1.[38] This was approved the same day by the NCL, and was supported at the conference by 2,413,000 votes to 170,000. Attlee made it clear that Labour was going in 'as partners and not as hostages'.[39] Thirdly, there is the dominating theme of the Labour leaders' speeches during the Commons debate – a trenchant accusation that the war was not being effectively prosecuted.[40]

'Labour, the War and the Peace' thus commanded the support of the Party as a whole – it was adopted overwhelmingly by a show of hands at the conference – and smoothed the ideological way for entry into the Coalition. Churchill himself played his part. His attitude to the war from the start expressed the predominant Labour sentiment in terms more vivid than those used by the Labour leaders. 'This is not a question of fighting for Danzig or Poland,' he had declared. 'We are fighting to save the whole world from the pestilence of Nazi tyranny and in defence of all that is sacred to man.'[41] The Labour leaders had been willing to meet Churchill and some other rebel Tories after Munich, and Churchill had also been agreeable.[42] As well, Edward Hyams has draw attention to a dialogue between Churchill and Kingsley Martin in the *New Statesman* in January 1939 which might have been designed to point out that this man, the one and only politician in whom Right and Left could find a war leader, need not be judged by the Labour Party on the undemocratic acts of his past, and that his very traditionalism, romanticism, Englishry, made him a good House of Commons man . . . In this dialogue . . . it was established that Churchill would, even in war-time, respect the House of Commons, maintain the freedoms which it guaranteed, tolerate free criticism of the executive . . . [43]

It remains to be noted that the only significant exception to the general unanimity which characterized the conference's acceptance of the NEC's statement was provoked by Dalton. He introduced the docu-ment to the delegates in a somewhat maladroit manner: 'We stand for a fight to the finish against Hitler and his gang,' he declared, and then added, 'If the German people will assist us, they will again be entitled to rank as human beings . . .'.[44] In using these words Dalton, though not quite exceeding his brief, allowed his bluntness to get the better of his discretion. The only attempt to modify the NEC's statement at the conference was directed more at Dalton than the statement itself. A resolution was introduced deploring the 'Fight to the Finish' attitude; it was easily defeated and this, in fact, was the means by which the document as a whole secured adoption. The incident foreshadowed, though, the prolonged moral debate on 'the German Question' which was to occupy much of the Party's time and energy during the war.

CHAPTER IV

Labour's Resolution put to the Test

May 1940–July 1941

LABOUR's twin resolution – to pursue the war against Nazi Germany, and to do this within the political framework of a national coalition government – soon received a two-fold test. In the first place there was the military crisis and its aftermath. The new government took office on the very day that Germany launched its attack on the West and the ensuing débâcle was unexpected. The climax of this phase may be said to have been reached during the first week of July 1940, with the British attack on the French fleet. The second 'test' was more complex; it focused on resurgence of the demand for 'war-aims', which was by no means confined to the Labour Party or even a segment of the Party. In one sense the demand represented the possibility of an extra weapon that the British could use in the prosecution of the war. Attlee himself, for a while, was inclined to this view. It also afforded Labour's Left wing an opportunity for developing its 'revolutionary' concept of the war. The demand could have taken another form – that of a renewed 'compromise peace' bid. Both aspects were complicated by the untried nature of the new government and its very mixed political composition.

From a numerical standpoint, in view of its slender parliamentary representation, Labour had little or nothing to complain of concerning the composition of the new administration. More important was Churchill's acceptance of the criticism that Attlee, and others, had made of the previous war cabinet's size; the new Prime Minister kept the foremost policy-making body extremely small throughout the war. Attlee was the only man, apart from Churchill himself, to serve in the war cabinet from the first day of the coalition to the last.* Bevin, along with Sir John Anderson, who was not formally attached to any

---

* The war cabinet on May 11, 1940, consisted of Churchill, Chamberlain, Attlee, Halifax and Greenwood; in May 1945 it consisted of Churchill, Attlee, Anderson, Bevin, Morrison, Lyttleton and Woolton.

political party, served for the next longest period and was the quickest of the Labour ministers to make his presence felt in terms of personality and power. Other Labour leaders who attained the highest level were Greenwood, Morrison and Cripps. The latter actually found himself in the war cabinet before he had been reinstated in the Labour Party. Dalton, though never a full member, attended when matters affecting his department were being considered (as did other ministers), and took great pains to keep himself informed, officially and unofficially, as his *Diaries* amply reveal.

Churchill's practical predominance in the field of foreign policy was greatest during the 1940–43 period. But at this time it was the military exigencies rather than the politics of the war which were the more pressing. Strategic decisions were naturally related to political apprecia-tions, but with the limited exception of Cripps there was little or no dispute with the Labour ministers over the former. In any case, until it became clear that the British were not merely not going to lose the war but that they would appear on the winning side, the relationship was of necessity a secondary consideration. After 1943, when the situation was reversed and the political aspect more important than the strategic, Labour's cabinet representation was stronger and its respon-sibility for the formulation of foreign affairs greater. Attlee and Cripps, in any case, were directly involved in diplomatic negotiations from the Coalition's earliest months and Bevin, through his close personal ties with Eden,[1] was equally influential. The strength of Attlee's position in the cabinet on foreign policy questions became apparent from February 1942 as a result of a contretemps with Beaverbrook.[2] In addition, Churchill proved 'most careful of his constitutional position and of constitutional practice',[3] as the *New Statesman* dialogue had intimated he would be. The war cabinet and Foreign Office were invariably consulted and, in the last analysis, the consent of Parliament obtained. Attlee's prior description of the Coalition as a 'partnership' was to be fully confirmed in foreign as well as domestic affairs – indeed, even more so in the former than the latter area. However, this was not clear to the Left, particularly at first.

The Left-wing's main complaint about the composition of the government was Churchill's retention in it of some leading figures from the previous administration, notably Chamberlain himself. Given the Prime Minister's own somewhat precarious political position at this time (Chamberlain remained leader of the Conservative Party until his death in 1941) and the critical urgency of the military situation, the Labour leaders were quite prepared to accept this temporary embarrassment, though not Churchill's proposed appointment of Chamberlain as Leader of the House.[4] Later, many of 'Chamberlain's men' were gradually eliminated or sent abroad. But this could never have happened quickly enough for the Left, who maintained a constant barrage of invective against the 'Men of Munich'. Ironically, fear of a compromise peace probably added now to general political antipathy. By December 1940 the Left's anxieties in this regard began to abate. Both the *New Statesman* and *Tribune* expressed the hope that Anthony Eden's appointment as Foreign Secretary that month foreshadowed the beginning of a new foreign policy.

The Coalition government got off to a good start so far as most Labour supporters were concerned. There were several reasons for this – the handling of the military crisis, Churchill's own enunciation of policy and his personal magnetism, and the government's initial domestic actions. The contribution of the Labour ministers to the first of these was quite positive. At the height of the Dunkirk crisis Attlee accompanied Churchill on the latter's second visit in June to France, in order to stiffen French resistance. The *Cabinet Papers*, from May to June, provide abundant evidence of Attlee's and Greenwood's determination to resist, even though some members of the new cabinet were still prepared to consider peace terms. The Labour leaders' view was that if Britain could survive until the end of the year it would suffice. Attlee, in particular, was convinced that Hitler had to win by this time as he was working to a timetable. Nor did the Labour leaders waver in their opposition to proposals from the French government that a direct approach to Italy be made by Britain and France. What Attlee wanted to see was the bombing of Germany.[5]

The Party, as a whole, approved. 'Are You a Traitor? Answer now' demanded Bevan in the *Tribune*; he could find only 'two tiny sections of the people who now doubt what is their duty ... the Extreme Left and the Extreme Right'.[6] It was either total victory or total defeat.[7] Laski claimed that 'the objective facts of the situation make a victory over Hitler a victory for Socialism'.[8] Victory, the priority on which Labour had just agreed, was precisely what Churchill – in inspiring words – offered; small wonder that he later recalled, 'In the early weeks it was from the Labour benches that I was mainly greeted.'[9] Bevan wrote of one of the great Churchillian set-pieces of this period: 'He was tremendous. History itself seemed to come into that chamber and address us. Nobody could have listened and not been moved.'[10] The speech referred to had been occasioned by the attack on the French fleet, with the clear implication that the government was bent on total war. In the case of most Labour members Churchill had been preaching to the converted. Reviewing the situation in August 1940, Harold Nicolson confided to his diary that a mood of defeatism or acquiescence could emerge in Britain, but consoled himself with the observation that, 'Fortunately the whole toughness and strength of this country seems to have passed into organized Labour. They are superb.'[11]

The Left had been given something else to applaud. The Emergency Measures Act of May 22, giving the government 'practically unlimited authority over all British citizens and their property'[12] boded fair to becoming the lynch-pin of the measures that the Left, and Attlee, deemed essential to the winning of the war and, by the Left to the winning of the peace also. The Act 'took everyone's breath away for a minute', *Tribune* commented.[13] The appointment of Cripps as Ambassador to the USSR, followed by his immediate despatch to Moscow, made a similarly favourable impression though, had the Left but known it, this action was not without a certain irony.[14]

Once France had fallen, of course, the question of how victory might eventually be secured, assuming Britain was not defeated or no compromise peace was arranged, required rather more than martial enthusiasm. The Labour ministers, in the obviously acute shortage of any immediate military solutions, toyed with some other ideas. Dalton, the Minister of Economic Warfare, wrote to Halifax in July that though, 'No doubt in the earlier part of the war the prospect of a revolution in Germany was remote ... The position in Europe is now completely different.' He pointed to anti-Nazi groups in the occupied countries and urged the creation of a special organization to foster and aid these groups. He wanted Attlee to run this organization, with help from himself, and wrote to Attlee accordingly the same day.[15] How seriously Dalton meant this is not clear, but at any rate, though Churchill 'was against Dalton taking over',[16] he was entrusted with the job. A Special Operations Executive (SOE) was established with the intention of making the enemy uncomfortable by every means: 'strikes, propaganda, terrorism, riots, boycott and bribery'.[17] But

Dalton soon became frustrated. 'Whenever I try to destroy anything anywhere I am caught in some diplomatic trip-wire' he complained to Halifax in December.[18]

Cripps's efforts were also doomed to disappointment. His arrival in Moscow, on June 12, was an unfortunate time for negotiations. There was little prospect of any substantial agreement, though that did not prevent Cripps from trying very hard to secure one. The Ambassador also fell foul of the Foreign Office. It is clear that he was willing to go much further than the latter in regard to the Russian absorption of the Baltic States.[19] But he was bound by his instructions – and there is no evidence of any discord about these on the part of the Labour ministers. They must have realized that Russian co-operation would depend more on further changes in the external situation than on anything else. Cripps remained undeterred, in spite of being pointedly informed by Molotov early in 1941 that Anglo-Soviet relations had become even worse since his arrival.[20] This was hardly his fault.

Attlee, in July, let it be known in government circles that an official pronouncement on future policy ought to be put before the country. The Germans were fighting a revolutionary war for very definite objectives: the British were fighting a conservative war with purely negative objectives. A positive and revolutionary aim ought to be formulated, admitting that the old order had collapsed and asking people to fight for a new one.[21] On August 23 the war cabinet agreed to set up a committee on War Aims – a decision which was implemented in October, with Attlee as chairman and Bevin as a member of the committee.[22] The committee at once agreed that there was a demand for a statement of general principles and objectives, and that it would be desirable to issue a statement as soon as possible.[23] Agreement on the terms of such a statement was another matter. The committee discovered that there was no shortage of material; in fact it was besieged with drafts and revisions of drafts from within and without government circles. Harold Nicolson, for instance, now Parliamentary Secretary to the Ministry of Information, prepared a paper which advocated a federal structure for post-war Europe and increasingly Socialist measures at home. Duff Cooper, his ministerial chief, agreed with Nicolson's draft (on which Halifax had collaborated) but feared it would create discord within the Coalition cabinet. This proved correct, and the main objection came from the Prime Minister. Churchill rejected the draft on the grounds that 'precise aims would be compromising, whereas vague principles would disappoint'.[24] The cabinet decided to postpone any statement,[25] and the committee on War Aims faded away. Even so, the Prime Minister's remarks in January, and his evident displeasure with Nicolson,[26] did not prevent Churchill from taking the initiative later in the year in the formulation of an equally vague set of principles, the Atlantic Charter.

Contrary to what the Left believed, Attlee's acquiescence in January 1941 owed little to personal 'weakness'. Though somewhat cautious by nature, he was not indecisive; the fact that, at certain times, he preferred to say nothing or to confine himself to generalities was deceptive. His silence was almost certainly the result of deliberate calculation and experience. His over-riding concern was that of maximum national political unity; his experience as chairman of the War Aims committee undoubtedly persuaded him that any immediate statement would do more harm than good in this respect. Such a tendency accorded with his experience as Leader of the Labour Party – a case in point being his failure to vote for 'Labour, the War and the Peace'. Now it was a question of Cabinet unity. Neither Labour's position in the government nor Churchill's were as yet secure. The only certainty in late 1940, and for most of the following year, was the menace of Germany and the Prime Minister's resolve not to give way before that menace. The close presence of the Chamberlainites would not have escaped Attlee. There was one other factor; the 'destroyers-for-bases' arrangement with the United States portended the possibility, at least, of vast future changes in the character of the war. Later in 1941, Attlee came to agree with Churchill's decision against stating war aims in a more positive way.

Outside government circles, and especially within Labour Party ranks, it was a different story. On August 31, 1940, the *New Statesman* published a letter appealing for a declaration of 'the objects for which this country fights' – not so much in detail as for 'the general principles on acceptance of which the war could be brought to an end'. Though acceptance by whom remained an unanswered question, the letter's significance lay in its fairly diverse group of signatories; these included H. G. Wells, Noel-Buxton, Laski, R. H. Tawney, Kingsley Martin, Lords Parmoor and Strabolgi, Leonard Woolf, Noel Brailsford, Arthur Creech-Jones MP, and Wilfred Roberts MP. What concerned them was not merely the absence of war aims, but the absence of 'revolutionary' war aims. This was the view even of such conservative newspapers as *The Times* and the *Daily Express*.[27] Inside the Labour Party the initiative was taken by Bevan and Laski.

Bevan urged the government to use their new powers to nationalize certain key industries – coal, railways, electricity – 'to provide the State with a sort of public backbone'.[28] Bevan's emergence during this period as Labour's leading parliament-based critic was mirrored by Laski outside the Commons: at the May annual conference of the Party, Laski headed the poll for membership on the NEC in the constituency section. It must be emphasized that Laski's first object remained the winning of the war. This, as well as his revolutionary concept of the war, had lain behind his pre-Coalition criticism of the Labour executive's attitude to Russia and his opinion of the electoral truce as a disaster. Foreseeing the eventual clash between Russia and Germany, Laski had declared to an American correspondent, the distinguished judge Felix Frankfurter, that it would be fatal for the British to range themselves against the Soviet Union, 'however badly Russia might behave in Poland, the Baltic States, or Finland'. He considered that 'Socialist purpose at home involved maintaining, even at great cost, a friendly attitude to the Soviet Union'.[29] After the German conquest of Western Europe Laski developed his theme of revolution more vigorously. At long last, he wrote, Great Britain had come to see that for her citizens it was now a question of victory or annihilation. Only a European revolution, however, could overthrow Hitler, and Great Britain had to take the lead in that revolution. She could do this by demonstrating that a just and equal society could be built even in the midst of war. Indeed, a democracy that was to wage total war had to end economic and social privilege as the price of victory.[30] The conflict, he insisted, was not only a struggle for world domination between old empires and new, it was also a declaration of bankruptcy on the part of capitalist civilization. It was not enough to want victory; it was essential to want victory for ends which would make possible an enduring peace.[31]

Literary and academic activities were one thing, an 'Open Letter to the Labour Movement' published in the *Daily Herald* quite another. This article, on October 27, 1940, constituted the climax of Laski's effort for the year; it resulted in a special meeting of the NEC 'for the purpose of putting little Laski on the mat', as Dalton described it.[32] The 'Open Letter' urged the Labour movement to demand war aims from the government. At the NEC meeting the would-be rebel agreed that his article had probably been unwise and liable to misrepresentation,[33] and this closed the incident so far as the Party was concerned. Afterwards, however, Attlee had a sharp personal word of rebuke for Laski; the Labour leader indicated that he was 'sufficiently experienced in warfare to know that the frontal attack with a flourish of trumpets, heartening as it is, is not the best way to capture a position'.[34] So chastened was Laski that he, in turn, wrote privately to the Prime Minister suggesting a continuation of the National government after the war, under Churchill's leadership. The object of this government would be the achievement of a comprehensive programme of social reform, as outlined by Laski.[35]

Bevan, also, was never a serious political threat, and probably knew it. The leadership took good care of its position; the potential political danger from those Labour MPs not in the government (who continued to sit on the opposition benches) was mitigated by the appointment of an acting and unpaid leader of the opposition chosen by the Labour ministers themselves. Other opposition front-benchers were elected by the PLP rump to form an administrative committee[36] whose main function, according to James Griffiths, a member of it, was two-fold; it was to sustain the Labour leaders in the government and to preserve the identity and unity of the Party.[37] Churchill himself later subscribed to the opinion that the latter purpose was achieved and, Bevan apart, the only other important parliamentary Labour rebel during the entire Coalition period was Emanuel Shinwell, whose disgruntlement was personal rather than political.[38] There were no serious disagreements in the Commons over foreign policy until 1944. Even over domestic issues, those Labour MPs not in the government divided the House but once, in 1943.

Stokes vainly continued to lead the Peace Aims Group. In July 1940 he wrote to Lloyd George 'on behalf of thirty MPs and ten Peers' to the effect that his Group was still prepared to negotiate with Hitler. Peace, Stokes reasoned, would restore prosperity which dictatorships could not survive.[39] By November he had joined the public clamour for a more explicit statement of war aims. Assuming that the only way the British could win the war was by means of a blockade, Stokes argued that this would ensure the economic collapse of Europe. Why should they destroy what they set out to save? he asked, meaning by this 'the rights of small nations'. Granting that if the Germans won there would be no question of a just peace, Stokes now maintained that the only feasible alternative was a declaration of war aims and a wait-and-see policy.[40] His Group did not support an amendment to the Address in December, by three ILP members, in favour of a negotiated peace.

There was another dimension to the frustrated demand for revolutionary war aims which became evident before the end of 1940. Bevan correctly identified this, in December, as the beginning of a 'great debate'. It could be said to centre around one issue, Bevan wrote:

> ... are we fighting the German people or the Nazis? Or to put it another way, have these calamities been brought upon Europe by something which is intrinsic in the nature of the German people or is it the product of German political institutions and of the German Nazi Party?[41]

The latter, of course, was the traditional 'Socialist' and, indeed, Labour answer, and it was this which Bevan re-affirmed. The distinction was becoming blurred in British, and Labour eyes; to some, later many, it seemed that there might be something in the old stories about German, and especially Prussian, militarism after all. Nevertheless, the propagation of Lord Vansittart's vehemently anti-German views, in a series of broadcasts in the last two months of 1940, came as something of a shock.[42] The *Daily Herald* treated the episode with caution, but made its underlying attitude clear enough in an editorial entitled 'Gift to Goebbels'.[43] By March 1941, the editor of *Tribune* felt obliged to state that 'Vansittart has started the equivalent of a plague, which is spreading rapidly. The damage that he has done is immensely greater than is understood in Left-wing circles.'[44]

One Labour leader, however, was quite unaffected, as he had never made any secret of his views on the issue. Hugh Dalton had, in March 1940, openly described Germany as 'the most regular and the most formidable trouble-maker in Europe' – for the past seventy years. Nazism was no isolated development: 'More rubbish about "racialism" had been talked, and taught, in Germany than anywhere else, long before this specially poisonous brand of current Nazi nonsense.' For good measure, Dalton had given strong hints of the kind of peace settlement he then had in mind. Before there could be any negotiations at all, there would have to be reparation. True, 'stupid blunders' had been made last time, but the paradoxical conclusion that the aggressor should be free from all obligations to pay damages had to be avoided.

As well, a satisfactory frontier settlement would involve transfer of population, which Dalton tactfully referred to in his book[45] as 'planned migration under fair conditions'. In private he was even more forth-coming. As Attlee perceived, he was a 'born intriguer';[46] his forte was the private conversation, discreet committee work and the subtle formulation of Party statements and resolutions. In July 1940, during a *tête-à-tête* luncheon with Ivan Maisky, the Russian Ambassador, he suggested that the Russians 'ought to arrange for an East Prussian Soviet Socialist Republic' – a suggestion that did not displease the Ambas-sador.[47] To W. Arnold Foster, a fellow-member of the NEC's Inter-national sub-committee Dalton explained in January 1941 that he was considering the creation of a South-Eastern European Confederation. Exchanges of populations were not merely desirable, but necessary. The underlying reason was that 'we cannot bear again that all the German tribes should stick together in a solid mass menacing all their neighbours'.[48] Nor was Dalton entirely alone in the Party in expressing these sentiments. A 'leading trade-unionist' told him in the same month that there should be no 'Germany' after the war, but a number of German states.[49]

Just prior to the Party's 1941 annual conference the NEC confirmed an earlier decision not to accept any resolutions on the subject of Germany's future.[50] The NCL renewed its appeal to the German workers in its May Day 'Manifesto', but this time a deliberate chal-lenge 'to renew the struggle for liberation' was included. At the conference, early in June, an ominous opening note was sounded by the president, James Walker MP. He informed the delegates that he 'was not one of those who, in this crisis, can separate the German people from the German Government'. On the contrary, he considered the German people just as responsible for the acts of their government as that government was itself. Furthermore, he attacked those who were 'quacking round the political pond' for a 'People's Convention' or a 'People's Government', and also the Peace Aimers. He demanded 'an overwhelming victory against the Germans . . . [who] must prove, after their defeat, that they could be trusted'.

Dalton had prepared a special memorandum, entitled 'The War and the Peace', which was submitted to the conference by the NEC in two parts. Both received overwhelming approval. There was little that was new in either of the statements, as they were designed to pro-duce the widest possible acceptance within the Party. Hence both statements made explicit reference to 'Socialist principles'; 'The War' stated that a growing acceptance of these would be necessary to secure an enduring peace, and 'The Peace' stated that the Party would press for their increasing application during the war. The clearest sections had to do with the necessity of victory and conversely the absurdity of a 'negotiated peace'. During the debate, two speakers (one of whom was Stokes) brought up the Vansittart question, but Noel-Baker, who replied for the executive, referred them to a recent speech by Eden which had emphasized that Vansittart's views did not represent government policy and that he was expressing a personal view.[51] However, the point about the conference that Dalton chose to record in his *Diary* was the 'Majority of more than 120 to 1 in favour of a total victory as a necessary prelude to a just peace'. He found a very good spirit had prevailed throughout the conference – to which he had done his best to contribute. Addressing the Society of Labour Candidates at a separate meeting, he had pleasantly informed them that Himmler had got the published list of their names, and that they would have a sticky time unless they won the war.[52]

Labour's twin resolution, mentioned at the beginning of this chapter, had thus met both aspects of the test. The government was well on the way towards becoming a true coalition and its single, or at least major, aim – the defeat of Germany – had survived intact. It had become clear that the Labour leaders shared, to a very large extent, the Churchillian view of the conflict and had thereby established their influence over policy. How that policy was to be achieved was not immediately apparent, but Labour's determination to achieve it had, if anything, increased. 'Standing alone', at any rate after October 1940, had not really been very dangerous; rather, it had been invigorating, even romantic. It had also revealed British impotence. Official Labour, after some casting around for an alternative, had had to be content – together with the cabinet – to wait upon events. These had not been slow in forthcoming. But the defeat of France, the blitz, and the increasing realization of Britain's inability to win unaided, had produced a major ideological problem: how to reconcile nationalist and Socialist ideas? Paradoxically, the Left's harassment and harping on the revolutionary theme may have contributed to this dilemma.

CHAPTER V

The Problem of Germany or the German Problem?

For the Left, the question of the Labour Party's attitude towards Germany was both one of political principle and also of Socialist morality: in Kingsley Martin's words, it was 'part of the problem of Europe and of our whole sick society'.[1] His paper gave a cautious welcome, in August 1941, to the Atlantic Charter on the grounds that 'To ignorant people who talk as if Germany could somehow be erased from the face of Europe, the Eight Points are a severe reverse'.[2] The following week, responding to a broadcast by the Prime Minister in which Churchill had said that Germany must be disarmed but not economically ruined, 'Critic' (Martin) argued that that policy did not correct the mistakes of the last Peace but repeated them. Apart from the folly of reparations, Churchill's proposals had, in effect, been carried out already, in 1919. Should they again want to maintain a situation in which they spent their substance on armaments while Germany developed economically, incidentally building up the basis of another war potential? 'Critic' could see no solution to the problem of Germany except in common economic institutions for Europe, ensuring general prosperity, and an international organization which would be responsible for policing Europe. In the second half of 1941, however, the Left tended to be on the defensive, emotionally, about Germany. They were inclined to stress 'realism' rather than ideology, and 'realism' included a preoccupation with the possibility of some kind of offensive military action.*

The way that Labour's mood was changing in more orthodox Party circles may be gathered from an article written by Bevin in November 1941. German preparation for the war, he declared in the *Daily Herald*, had started long before Hitler. Even if they 'got rid of Hitler, Goering and others', he warned, that would not end the German problem.

---

* See Chapter VI.

'It was Prussian militarism, with all its terrible philosophy, that had to be got rid of from Europe for all time.'[3] Inside the Party a move had already begun to bring about a drastic change in official policy. Some time in October 1941, the chief of the International Department, who was also the secretary to the NEC's sub-committee on International Affairs, prepared a document entitled 'German Social Democracy: Notes on Its Foreign Policy.'[4] It purported to demonstrate historically that no German, not even a Social Democrat, could be entrusted with power. The author, William Gillies, was a diminutive Scot from Glasgow, who had been appointed to his post in the International Department as long ago as 1919. Emanating from a person for so long associated with the Party bureaucracy and of such high standing in it, the 'Notes' in themselves provide a significant example of the emerging mood. This significance is doubled in the case of Gillies, for he had personally gone to considerable trouble in aiding many German Socialists to reach Britain and to establish themselves once arrived.[5] The story of what happened to his document within Party circles is still more indicative of the growing Labour bitterness towards Germany.

Considering that the 'Notes' took the form of an historical survey, there could have been few people in the Party better equipped to refute them than Philip Noel-Baker, who had been actively involved in international affairs, particularly at the League of Nations, ever since the Versailles settlement. He and Gillies had often jointly participated at international political gatherings, especially of European Socialists, on Labour's behalf. Hardly a year had elapsed since Noel-Baker, Gillies and Laski had seen Morrison, the Home Secretary, in order to request that German and Austrian political refugees be recognized as such and be released from internment.[6] In November 1941, Noel-Baker's concern, which he expressed in a memorandum, went beyond the question of Gillies's historical scholarship. (Laski described this 'scholarship' in a letter to Noel-Baker as 'a perverse and distorted account of the facts' about which no scholar 'could have any feelings but consternation'.) It was, rather, the purpose of Gillies's 'Notes' which mostly engaged Noel-Baker. Whatever had happened a quarter of a century ago, the salient fact for him was that 'German Social Democracy is at present unanimously against the Nazis . . . its leaders are working for the defeat of Nazi Germany and . . . they are therefore a potential ally who deserve the highest consideration'. The 'Notes' raised the question of 'whether Mr Gillies is in accord with Party policy about Germany'. Nor did they stand alone; they were 'related to a number of other episodes which have happened in recent months . . .'.[7] Noel-Baker's intuition was substantiated by events. Gillies and a number of associates were intent on changing Labour's official position from what, in their eyes, was a 'soft' approach to a 'hard-line' one.

Quite unmoved by the hostile reaction of Noel-Baker and Laski, Gillies proceeded to amass further commentaries on his 'Notes' from the various German Socialist emigré groups and individuals in London. All of these, together with a copy of the original document, Noel-Baker's memorandum and Laski's letter, were widely circulated by Gillies, especially among members of the NEC. The result, Dalton noted, was a 'first-class row' at a meeting of the NEC's International sub-committee in November 1941. Dalton himself, playing an altogether more subtle game than Gillies, attempted to pour 'a little oil on the troubled waters . . .',[8] but the episode, far from ending there, was merely beginning. By 1942 an independent pressure group had appeared on the Labour scene; Fight For Freedom Editorial and Publishing Services Ltd informed the secretary of the Labour Party in February that the Company would work in the immediate future 'to provide more complete and accurate knowledge of the historical events in Germany which [had led] Europe again into war'.[9] In fact, the main aim of 'Fight For Freedom' was to persuade the British Labour movement that the responsibility for the war lay not merely with the Nazi Party but, even more, with the Germans. The new group was to make its biggest impact on the trade union side, but with Gillies already waging his own propaganda campaign from within the Party bureaucracy it was soon clear to the Left that they had another domestic opponent on their hands, besides Mr Churchill.

Unlike Gillies, Fight For Freedom did not confine its activities to working behind the scenes; instead it deliberately courted publicity and hastened to follow Vansittart's example in method and matter. A furious literary controversy ensued, which saw various Party and Left-wing figures pitted against each other.[10] The somewhat mysterious founder and managing director of the group, Walter Loeb, challenged the *New Statesman* to explain how Germany's industrial potential should be employed after the war. The paper replied that the destruction of German heavy industry would involve the impoverishment of Germany and the civilized world as a whole. The real question was that of the economic organization of the post-war world, though it might be that German, as well as British and American industry, would have to adapt itself to new conditions. As regards German industry in particular, the guarantees, other than those of full employment and disarmament, which would be relied upon, would include a German social revolution, some quasi-federal organization of Europe, an international force, and international control of strategic raw materials. The paper felt, however, that to go into details at the present time would be 'to engage in pipe-dreams in the dark'. It was content to lay down a general principle – that after the colossal destruction of the war, 'the central aim of civilized men should be to conserve and utilise to the full every instrument, in Germany and elsewhere, by which the world's wealth can be built up and its distribution fairly planned'.[11]

Meanwhile, what may be called the affair of Gillies's 'Notes' continued to simmer in the NEC's International sub-committee. To George Dallas, who was chairman of the committee, Gillies wrote in February that his 'Notes' stood 'in no need of correction, even in detail'. He had 'nothing to extenuate and nothing to withdraw'.[12] When it met, a few days later, the sub-committee fell into another heated argument on the matter – much to Dalton's distaste; he described it as 'a long discussion about German refugees and who has said what about whom'.[13] In March, when the nature of German Social Democracy again appeared on the sub-committee's agenda, James Walker MP, a former chairman of the Party, moved a specific resolution. This stated that, after study, the committee

> are of the opinion that the document of Mr William Gillies is true in all essentials, and that the charge contained in Mr Noel-Baker's document that Mr Gillies is out of line with the Party Policy is entirely without foundation.[14]

This resolution was carried by 4 votes to 2, and as Noel-Baker and Laski were both present it is a safe assumption that theirs were the opposition votes. Two other members of the committee were also present, and presumably abstained. During the following month the issue went before the full NEC, in spite of an attempt by Mrs Ayrton-Gould and Shinwell to postpone the matter. The sub-committee's decision was debated in two resolutions put to the vote: (1) that Gillies's 'Notes' were true in all essentials and (2) that Noel-Baker's charge was entirely without foundation. Both were carried, the first by an 8 to 5 majority, the second by 10 to 3.[15] As at least twenty-six members of the NEC were present (though not Attlee), a large number abstained from voting on both counts. The fact that they did so is further evidence of the extent of anti-German feeling within the Party at this time.

The previous month a formal attempt had been made by a small group of Labour activists to denounce the 'Fight For Freedom' campaign and to link it with Gillies. Leading members of this group included Austin Albu, who became post-war political adviser to the British military government in Germany, and Patrick Gordon-Walker, a future Labour Foreign Secretary. The Socialist Clarity Group published a monthly series of *Labour Discussion Notes*[16] and the March issue described the real purpose of the Fight For Freedom Company as being 'to propagate the kind of views regarding Germany which have been associated with the name of Lord Vansittart'. Walter Loeb, had 'no great record as a fighter against Nazism', yet he had contrived to get himself 'accepted as a suitable colleague by prominent members of the British Labour Movement', of whom there were many 'prepared to accept the word of Mr W. Gillies . . .'. The article gave rise to a whole series of charges and counter-charges, and was brought before the NEC at the same April meeting, when the question of Gillies's 'Notes' was considered. It was resolved that the attack upon Gillies was unjustified; the NEC formally expressed its entire confidence in him![17]

In 1942, official Labour tried to avoid adding further public fuel to this ideological fire smouldering in the literary and political underbrush. *Labour Looks Ahead*, a Party pamphlet published in March, was only slightly more specific than previous statements about post-war policy. The Allies would have to maintain armed forces after the war, as the years of transition would be difficult, it warned. A 'permanent Peace system would have to be based on two foundations; co-operation between Great Britain, the United States, the USSR and China; and the destruction of the social and economic bases of militarism in the aggressor nations'. Another Party publication[18] insisted that not only must there be no peace with the dictators, but that 'the peoples of Germany, Italy and Japan must be brought finally to realise that the power which the peace-loving nations can mobilise against aggression is overwhelming'. True, the NCL in its May Day 'Manifesto' again appealed to the German (and, this time, the Italian) workers,[19] but this proved to be the last such appeal.

The annual conference, held in May, also played down the German issue. In retrospect, the most interesting aspect of the debate on international affairs in this connection lies in the remarks of J. B. Hynd, who was to be the first post-war Labour minister in charge of the British zone in Germany. Hynd moved an addendum to a number of rather flowery resolutions proposed for the NEC by Noel-Baker. He called for a report setting out in detail the Party's views on the post-war reconstruction of Europe, 'based on their past resolutions and on their Socialist principles'. Hynd described the NEC resolution relating to the European problem as 'confined entirely to greetings and assurances of fellowship'. To the ordinary worker this was 'so much political mumbo-jumbo', yet 'The suppression of the Junkers and the nationalization of the basic heavy industries of Germany and other capitalist countries' would be something those same workers would understand. Hynd was a 'soft-liner' on Germany and hoped to commit the Party to a specific policy.[20]

Prior to the conference, the NEC had been rather pleased at the 'political mumbo-jumbo'; it had 'expressed immense admiration' for the International resolution which had been drafted by Dalton, Gillies and Hugh Gaitskell.[21] Noel-Baker, who replied to Hynd's strictures, claimed that the central committee on Reconstruction (set up after the 1941 conference) was doing precisely what Hynd demanded. But he did not dwell on the fact that the International sub-committee of the Reconstruction committee was chaired by George Dallas, a leading advocate of a 'hard-line' German policy. Either the 'insiders' of both persuasions judged the moment not altogether ripe for a detailed public dispute or, as Kingsley Martin claimed, the Party was paralysed between the Internationalists and Vansittartites on the executive. They cancelled each other out, and the result was evasion of the chief problem of the morrow.[22]

Although the Labour Party's annual conference soft-pedalled the German issue, the same was not true of the TUC's annual meeting held in September. The president delivered a withering attack on 'Those who profess and plead for sympathy for the German people...' He hated to say it, but he was convinced

... that until the German people, not alone their gangster rulers, have meted out to them what they have meted out to millions of their fellow-creatures . . . the German people will again, if not prevented . . . make another attempt to enslave Europe.[23]

The same month the NEC published its endorsement of a resolution that had been forwarded to it in July by the International sub-committee stating that

. . . the British Labour Movement has heard with indignation and horror of the organized and bestial atrocities committed by Germany in Poland and Czechoslovakia . . . [and that these] . . . cast infamy on those who have perpetrated them and dishonour upon the nation which has acquiesced in them.[24]

News of these atrocities probably contributed to the renewal of the debate over 'the German issue' which occurred in the autumn of 1942.

The 'hardliners', especially the Fight For Freedom Group, came under fire from a number of quarters. A monthly journal, *Socialist Commentary* (not a Left-wing publication) accused the Group, in September, of poisoning the atmosphere in internationalist circles, though admitting that it was now 'an open secret that on the most vital questions of European policy there is a deep cleavage in the leading circles of Labour'. The debate fairly saturated the editorial pages and correspondence columns of the Left-wing papers. H. G. Wells wrote to both *Tribune*[25] and the *New Statesman*[26] defending Vansittart. Laski replied[27] and was, in turn, rebuked by the historian, A. L. Rowse: 'One had to be either very clever or very silly,' Rowse declared, 'not to be able to see that something is dangerously wrong with the Germans. Ordinary people . . . whose point of view has been expressed by Mr Wolstencroft, President of the TUC, not by the Laskis and the Gollanczes, appreciate this perfectly well.'[28] *Tribune* devoted an editorial specifically to criticism of Vansittart.[29] Bernard Shaw, inevitably, had his own point of view; he found Vansittart and Wells 'amusing'.[30] The Fight For Freedom Group remained impervious to all adverse comment and – if anything – redoubled its activities. A round table conference at the Savoy Hotel in London was organized in December 1942, and was addressed by Greenwood and another influential Labour figure, A. J. Dobbs. A flood of letters from constituency parties enquiring or protesting about this conference which reached Gillies[31] (in his official capacity) was doubtless ignored.

None of this had any effect on Dalton; nor did he permit the vicissitudes of the military situation to affect his post-war thinking. August 1942 was perhaps the darkest month of all: although Rommel had been temporarily stopped, El Alamein was still some two months away; the German tide flowed remorselessly on in southern Russia, reaching the Volga before the end of the month, and the northern convoys were in serious trouble. At the very moment when the possibility of a German victory was most formidable, Dalton composed a long and secret memorandum on 'Reparations',[32] which rejected any notion that the pursuit of the latter was rationally or morally disreputable. The previous muddle had been unnecessary; morally there was no limit, in his opinion, to what it would be just to claim from Germany. Nor was there any virtue in 'moderation', either in doing justice or in taking steps to prevent a repetition of German crime. He hoped that no one would boggle at 'interferences' in German economic and financial life. Moreover, British export prospects would be brighter in a Europe 'in which Germany was largely disindustrialized while other States, particularly in Eastern Europe, were industrialized'.

By November he was able to note with satisfaction that both Cripps and Attlee appeared to favour his point of view. In a paper on a proposed 'Four Power Plan' (which will be referred to again later), Cripps identified the main danger to European peace as stemming from the strong and central position of Germany with her large population and industries. Though Cripps was against any financial indemnity, he did think that reparation should be exacted in the form of repair and replacement. Ultimately the safety of Europe would depend upon Germany being less powerful economically while her neighbours were more powerful.[33] In a private note to Eden about the 'Four Power Plan', Dalton stressed that 'Germany is, and will remain, even though defeated, the greatest potential danger to the world's peace and the lives of our children. It is our primary duty to break her power for evil deeds, now and through the long future.'[34] In the same month, Dalton found that Attlee 'would take away all machine tools from Germany and distribute them among her victims, Poles, Czechs, Russians, etc.'.[35] As well, Dalton kept close watch upon the activities of the first committee of officials[36] which had been established to solicit and consider various expert reports on reparations and economic security. He was quite clear, he told his own Board of Trade officials on the committee in November, 'that the power of Germany to

66

prepare and make war must be greatly weakened and that this [was] both a British interest, a European interest and, indeed, an interest of all humanity'. Dalton suggested to his ministerial colleague Kingsley Wood, the Chancellor of the Exchequer, that he should 'rub into Keynes the need to weaken Germany so much that she will be industrially unable to repeat her crimes in future'.[37]

General Labour feeling on the subject at the end of 1942 may best be gauged, perhaps, by two separate incidents. An official Party deputation to the Foreign Secretary in December was composed of both 'hard' and 'soft-liners':[38] the object of their visit was the German persecution of the Jews. A subsequent NEC statement described this as 'the bloodiest crime in history' and declared that such an 'unparalleled and stupendous act of barbarism will always be associated with the name of modern Germany'.[39] The second incident concerned the International sub-committee of the NEC which, by January 1943, had drawn up a report entitled 'Armistice'.[40] Though it assumed the total defeat of the Axis Powers, the report also stated that:

> . . . either the will, the energy, the technical resources of the Germans will become harnessed voluntarily before very long to purposes which are compatible with the survival of a Europe peaceful and free, or else this war will have been fought in vain.

In addition the hope was expressed that as regards the repatriation of enemy prisoners, the 'harsh and embittering policy' followed in 1919 would not be repeated, though some payment of reparations and restitution would be 'right and practicable' so long as any such measures did not prejudice the general recovery of the world's prosperity. This report was never published, its tone being clearly alien to the Party's new mood.

The twelve months which had elapsed since the war against Germany had been transformed into a world-wide struggle – with all its political implications – had also witnessed a profound change in Labour's emotional response to the war. To a large and increasing extent the problem of Germany had become the German problem, though this had not yet received official Party sanction. Nor had the changed mood made any material impact upon the post-war policy actually advocated in the Cabinet by the Labour ministers. But there was a simple explanation for this; such discussions had scarcely moved as yet beyond the most tentative of levels and were still of secondary concern. Moreover, the international political situation had become immeasurably more complex and problematical. When the time did arrive for such discussions, however, the effect of the Labour Party's new attitude, as interpreted and shared by the Labour ministers, was to become quite evident.

CHAPTER VI

Labour and the War, 1941–43

FROM 1941 to 1943 the crucial question was not so much that of Germany's future as of Britain's. It is true that the last six months of 1941 witnessed a transformation in the character of the war. In retrospect, the German attack on Russia, together with Hitler's declaration of war on the United States, ultimately ensured the defeat of Germany. But this was by no means so clear at the time; the significance of these changes was potential rather than actual. Until the German tide was decisively turned in Russia in 1943 the result of the war remained a matter of considerable doubt. Had Russia succumbed quickly, as was generally believed possible and, in the beginning, even probable, the entire military might of Germany could have been directed against Britain before the United States could have materially affected the situation. Concern for the way Britain was 'fighting' the war was to be heard in all political circles; in the Labour Party such concern was widespread.

As the German invasion pushed into Russia during the second half of 1941, Bevan, *Tribune* and Shinwell were increasingly taken up with the possibility that some kind of offensive action might be mounted and if so, mounted directly against Germany. Bevan, in the summer, urged that then was the moment to strike, if not with an expeditionary force (and he suspected not) at least by 'a series of raids, never aiming at permanent occupation, but always carrying the threat of it . . .' Germany would have to maintain troops and equipment against the possibility that one of the raids might develop.[1] He brought his criticism of the British military effort to the floor of the Commons in October,[2] when he received the somewhat unexpected support of Noel-Baker. But the most penetrating remarks were made by Shinwell in November. Anticipating the British attack in the Western Desert by five days, he asked derisively if the government's strategy was to be limited 'to guarding the Empire lines of communication, particularly of the Eastern Empire, the creation of an eastern Maginot line?' This might seem attractive, but it was fatal if the intention was the achievement of victory. Nor was it certain that, by placing large forces in the Middle East, the best safeguard could be provided. 'Diversions elsewhere may prove to be more effective,' he too suggested. Above all, it was important to establish whether the government regarded the defence of the eastern Empire as a second front, and if so, whether the idea met with the approval of the Russian government. Shinwell concluded his speech with an attack on the organization of the home front. A. V. Alexander, the Labour First Lord of the Admiralty, who was put up to reply for the government, was reduced to personal disparagement of his fellow Party member.[3]

Shinwell's main point was well made, though the Labour Party as a whole had not objected to the campaign in the Middle East in 1940, nor to the ill-fated Greek campaign earlier in 1941.[4] The truth of the matter at this time, despite America's entry into the war, was that the British government had no clear idea as to how the war might be won. The eastern front 'was not seen as a theatre where the final decision would be reached'.[5] Attlee and Bevin fully shared the doubts – which Cripps came to express by the beginning of 1942 – about 'Russia's ability to withstand an attack of the *blitzkrieg* variety which had overcome the great French army within a month'.[6] On the other hand, the government did have ideas as to where the war might be lost. Reviewing the situation in July 1942, Churchill emphasized that the most salient feature was 'the immense power of the German military machine'. Almost equally important was the question of sea-borne tonnage.[7] Even so, the Prime Minister had toyed with the possibility of mounting some kind of offensive action in northern France to relieve Russia, as late as March 1942 – much to the irritation of his chief military adviser, Sir Alan Brooke.[8] But, quite apart from this (and Churchill was probably not serious), the cry for a second front in 1942 was not universal. True, the Russians wanted it, and the Americans favoured it. Some important officials such as Sir Alexander Cadogan, the head of the Foreign Office, were converted to it.[9] Inside and, subsequently, outside, the war cabinet, Lord Beaverbrook strenuously advocated it.[10] The Labour Left clamoured for it. The Labour cabinet ministers remained impervious.

There was one, over-riding reason for this attitude; the Labour ministers, like Churchill, accorded top priority to imperial defence.

They were naturally aware of the Anglo-American strategic decision of 'Germany First', originally agreed in staff talks between January and March 1941[11] and confirmed at the top-level Arcadia Conference held in Washington between December 1941 and January 1942. The war cabinet also decided in April 1942 that preparations for operations should go ahead without delay.[12] This, however, was merely a temporary obeisance to American views. Earlier in April, Attlee had been present in his regular capacity as a member of the Defence Committee (Operations) of the war cabinet,* and had heard the Americans present their plan for a second front. Churchill had accepted it, subject to one reservation – the defence of India and the Middle East. Attlee agreed; the plan had ushered in a new phase of the war. Hitherto they had been hanging on to the best of their ability and with few resources. Now the time had arrived to wrest the initiative from the enemy. At the same time, he added significantly, they had great responsibilities in other parts of the world, and it was entirely right that they should safeguard these while concentrating the main striking force in the European theatre.[13] Attlee, too, put the defence of the Empire rather than the liberation of Europe first.

A vital British strategic consensus emerged during the spring of 1942, which received formal confirmation by the cabinet in June – during, that is, Molotov's visit to London. It was then decided that there would be no substantial landing in France that year unless (*a*) it was to be permanent, and (*b*) the Germans had been previously demoralized by failure against Russia.[14] Thus the landing in Europe to 'help' the Russians would depend on a prior Russian victory. Though determined to see Germany defeated, the Coalition cabinet apportioned the prime responsibility for bringing this about to the Russians. The eastern front *was* the decisive one. Now at last it had become meaningful to talk about 'a fight to the finish'! This decision, one of the most significant of the entire war, was not communicated as such to either of the major Allies.† It was fraught with implications and attended by

---

* Attlee served as chairman of this committee in the absence of Churchill.

† An *aide-memoire* handed to Molotov on the previous day stated that though preparations were being made for an invasion of the Continent in August and September, the main limiting factor was the availability of landing craft, and thus no promise could be given. However, the Russians were assured that the maximum effort was being concentrated on the organization and preparation of a large-scale invasion of the Continent by British and American forces in 1943, and that no limit was to be set to this operation. (CAB 65/30).

consequences of the greatest political as well as military importance. For the moment it will suffice to note that the decision led directly, though not perhaps inevitably, to the postponement of the second front and to the eventual Anglo-American adoption of a 'Mediterranean strategy'.

There were, of course, entirely pragmatic and opportunistic grounds both for the June decision and for the more specific development of the 'Mediterranean strategy' which followed the Casablanca Conference, in January 1943. Underlying these (from the British point of view) were the six months of successive defeats in 1942 and the memory of the disastrous experience during the First World War. *Tribune*'s military correspondent indicated his awareness of the latter, which was widely shared on the Left in November 1942; then, after El Alamein and the North African landing, the British had gained a measure of military success. 'At last,' he wrote, 'we have engaged in the strategy of the indirect approach by which all our wars, except the last, have been won with least cost and therefore more profit to ourselves.'[15] During the first half of 1942, however, while Russia bled and burned and the British seemed to mark time, the advantages of the 'indirect' or 'limited liability' approach were certainly not apparent to the British Left or, for that matter, to those of different political persuasions.

Returning from his visit to Washington, in January 1942, the Prime Minister made no bones about the matter and demanded a vote of confidence precisely because things had gone badly, and worse was to come. Where would they have been, he questioned, if they had yielded to the clamour of a few months ago and had invaded France or the Low Countries? This point was well-taken by the spokesman for the official Labour opposition, F. W. Pethick-Lawrence (in place of the recently deceased H. B. Lees-Smith). He made it clear that he had 'no use whatever for captious criticism of the Prime Minister and the Government'. This did not prevent Shinwell from referring to the 'steady and deplorable deterioration in the war situation' in the past few weeks. He rejected Churchill's argument that the Far East had been denuded of supplies in favour of Russia. He criticized the governmental structure, and especially its effect on production.[16] In making this last point, Shinwell was on firmer or, at least, less controversial ground, as was conceded by the government soon after the debate. Attlee felt obliged to admit that there had been a 'real debate', but described Shinwell as 'the greatest optimist in the House'. Attlee blunted the issue by insisting that the vote of confidence did not imply that the government's personnel was the best possible, or that everyone was always satisfied with everything the government had done. The vote was obtained by 464 votes to 1, only a solitary member of the ILP actually voting against, though obviously there were some deliberate abstentions.

On both Left and Right sides of the political spectrum discontent continued to simmer. Cripps, returning politically untarnished from Moscow, refused an immediate offer of the Ministry of Supply and referred publicly in February to the lack of urgency in the country.[17] Beaverbrook, making a bid for power that same month, terminated his cabinet appointment and appeared to prove that the second front issue could unite the political extremities.[18] Both fell foul of the two leading Labour cabinet ministers, whose influence was thereby strengthened. Beaverbrook's bid foundered on the joint opposition of Attlee and Bevin,[19] while Cripps's prospects of further advancement were blocked, at first, by Attlee alone.[20] That Cripps was subsequently appointed to the war cabinet was due to Attlee's realization that Cripps, in one respect, had changed his views. It is highly probable, also, that Churchill and Attlee deemed Cripps less of a liability in the cabinet than out of it. Criticism of the government's military conduct of the war continued and Cripps was soon called upon to defend it.[21]

The climax of this stage of the Coalition's political difficulties was reached in July 1942. A Commons debate on a motion by Sir John Wardlaw-Milne that, while recognizing the heroism of the armed forces, the House had 'no confidence in the central direction of the war', was seconded by another Conservative MP, Admiral of the Fleet Sir Roger Keyes. The details of this debate have been too often cited to require much additional comment here. The first Labour member to support the motion, Fred Bellenger, complained about 'the pressure to which Labour members [had been] subjected from their own party'. For the official opposition, Greenwood limited himself to asking that the government explain why the British had been defeated in Libya. The most notable contribution to the debate by the Labour rebels came from Bevan, but even his brilliant debating speech[22] could not save the government's critics from the ridicule attached to them as the result of Wardlaw-Milne's celebrated gaffe – the suggestion that the Duke of Gloucester be made commander-in-chief. Bevan did, however, achieve a more precise formulation of Labour criticism. He produced three specific charges: 'First, the main strategy of the war has been wrong; second, the wrong weapons have been produced; and third, those weapons are being managed by men who have not studied the use of modern weapons.' In addition, he claimed that Churchill had not understood the nature of the weapons used by the enemy since the beginning of the war. And he concluded with an appeal for a second front: 'Get at the enemy where he really is – twenty-one miles away . . .'.[23] Given the organized Party support, the vote was a foregone conclusion, 25 for the motion, 476 against, with some 40 deliberate abstentions but, as A. J. P. Taylor remarks, 'the cloud was still there. Churchill had to produce success, not a majority in the voting lobbies.'[24]

As well as the second front issue, the widespread impression during much of 1942 that the war was not being effectively prosecuted provided a strong impetus to a marked revival of Party feelings. Frustrated by Britain's apparent inability to do anything very significant about Germany, many members of the Labour Party were attracted, instead, to domestic issues. By the end of the year Attlee, according to one of his assistants, had become 'very conscious of difficulties in the Party'.[25] Those Labour MPs not in the government manifested their grievances on several occasions in the Commons. In December 1941, some 35 of them insisted on carrying to a division an amendment to the Manpower Bill, demanding that property as well as men and women should be conscripted, and that the transport, coal-mining and munitions industries should be nationalized. But only eight of these actually voted for the amendment,[26] just as only eight Labour MPs had voted against the government on the non-confidence motion in July.[27] Still, the discontent was certainly there. Harold Nicolson believed that the vote of some 63 Labour members against the government later in July on an Old Age Pensions bill reflected the agitation on the second front question.[28] And the major revolt of the entire war occurred in February 1943 over the Beveridge Report when – with only two exceptions – all Labour MPs not in office voted for stronger approval of the Report.

The general unrest served to encourage and embolden the Left. Many middle-class Socialists joined the new CommonWealth Party, which was founded in 1942 by Sir Richard Acland.[29] But on one significant issue – that of Indian self-government – the Left was obliged to reverse what had hitherto been one of its most basic demands. Cripps's mission to India altered the situation. Though *Tribune* believed it proper that the Indian leaders should try to obtain the utmost concessions from the British government, the paper now suggested that the Indians should not insist on '. . . crossing the Ts and dotting the Is of proposals which [appeared] . . . to form a reasonable basis for complete Indian self-government'. It was hoped that these same leaders would not play into the hands of the most reactionary British elements by holding out for conditions that the war situation made it difficult, if not impossible, to give.[30] This was a dubious argument. It could be, and was, used by the Labour leadership against the Left on domestic questions. By the autumn, *Tribune* directed its attack with greater vehemence against the Labour leaders themselves, even having a word of reproach for its erstwhile standard-bearer. Cripps had been too loyal, too selfless, too patriotic and too politically innocent.[31] There was more to it than that. A few days before Cripps had said that:

> . . . broadly speaking, those who join in the united effort from what is generally referred to as the political Left cannot expect in the present circumstances that the Government should introduce legislation merely for the purpose of bringing about a complete change in our political and economic structure.[32]

This was just what the Left *did* expect. Bevan argued that Labour must reconsider its position in the Coalition, even if actual victory was still far away. He doubted whether the presence of Labour in the government was any longer necessary for national unity, though if it were, he would continue to support the Coalition, as the defeat of Hitler remained the most important priority.[33]

The latter, of course, was the leadership's ideological trump card, though they were prepared and to some extent obliged to do battle on other grounds also. 'This is a people's war,' Ernest Bevin pronounced in the spring, 'it must lead to a people's peace.'[34] The various measures of what has been called 'War Socialism' were increasingly necessary and inevitable from 1942 onwards because of a virtual manpower budget. They were personified by Bevin himself, now at the height of his power, and actually provoked a (successful) revolt by Right-wing Conservatives over a proposed fuel-rationing scheme. 'Our Party has not lost its identity . . .' asserted the chairman of the annual conference, in May.[35] The greatest single thorn in the leadership's flesh during the year was Laski, the Left's most articulate ideological protagonist. In March 1942, he wrote to his friend Felix Frankfurter in the United States that, fearing Churchill intended to preserve traditional Britain, he (Laski) would henceforth try to make the Labour Party break with Churchill on this issue.[36]

That same month the question of Party unity became the subject of a joint meeting of the NEC and the executive committee of the PLP. Greenwood drew up a memorandum which purported to define more precisely the role of the official Labour opposition in the Commons in relation to its general support of the war effort. Three main areas of activity were identified: (1) representing to the government, and particularly to Labour members of it, opinions, grievances and defects in the organization and administration; (2) bringing to bear on the government constructive criticism and suggestions with a view to the more effective prosecution of the war; and (3) keeping in the forefront, in order to fortify the national morale, their primary peace aims. Clearly, this set strict limits on the opposition, but anything closer to the role of a formal opposition, Greenwood believed, would soon bring the Party out of the government.[37] Laski was not satisfied and prepared a criticism of Greenwood's memorandum in time for the next NEC meeting. Attlee now intervened. Together with his colleagues in the government, he said, he took the view 'that the Labour Party should not try to get Socialist measures implemented under the guise of winning the war . . .'. Laski, Attlee correctly considered, 'was prepared to insist upon a minimum programme of measures being demanded from the Prime Minister, even at the risk of breaking up the government'. In that case, Attlee demanded, 'What would be the effect on the Party if, in fact, it left the Government? . . . it would be held that the Party had slipped out of responsibility when things looked black.' This intervention appears to have been decisive; no formal vote was taken.[38]

At the 1942 annual conference, Party unity in the face of the critical war situation was the main theme. The chairman, Alderman W. H. Green, a Co-operative movement figure, set the tone in his opening address; he hoped that 'no spirit of defeatism or disunity would mar the Conference'. Not only was unity in the country vital, but the Party had a right to expect the same unity among the parliamentary Party. Though Attlee attempted to minimize the conflicts and maximize support for 'the necessity of achieving total victory over our enemies', he did not altogether succeed. An amendment was moved which would have had the effect of declaring that Labour should end its association with the Coalition. The argument was put forward that though man-power had been organized efficiently, other elements had not and that the Conservatives were taking Party advantages. Winding up the debate for the executive, Herbert Morrison judged the moment ripe for a tongue-lashing. After speaking of 'the achievements of the Labour ministers' he declared that

> This Party is never happy when it is in government . . . because the Party has got too much of the mind of perpetual opposition . . . too much of the perpetual minority complex, and because some of you have too much of the perpetual inferiority complex as well . . .

The amendment was duly defeated, by some 164,000 votes to 2,319,000.

Laski had the duty, or penance, of speaking for the executive at the conference. On its behalf he moved a vague resolution favouring no return after the war to an unplanned competitive society, etc. The resolution concluded that it was urgent to undertake without delay the necessary preparation for the vital changes proposed. How tame this must have appeared to him! He referred, in the course of his speech, to the war as revolutionary; he insisted that Churchill should recognize that the military defeat of Hitler in itself was not enough, that the forces of production had to be liberated, and that the war was equally against vested interests at home and abroad. Laski again topped the poll for membership of the NEC in the constituency section of the ballot, being followed by Shinwell. Even more disturbing to the leadership and indicative of Party feeling was the debate on parlia-mentary by-elections. Here the executive's proposal was simply that the electoral truce be continued. Bevan, and others, vigorously opposed this and moved that it be referred back to the executive. This was only defeated by the slenderest of margins, 1,275,000 votes to 1,209,000.[39]

Shortly after the conference, Laski made public his disagreement with his fellow NEC members. He, too, called for an end to the truce. He alleged that, under the guise of avoiding controversial questions, 'Mr Churchill is, in fact, being allowed to determine the economic destiny of this country after victory . . .'.[40] It was not so much this article, though, as one in the popular paper, *Reynolds News*, which resulted in yet another appearance by Laski before an NEC meeting in October. There, he indicated that he was prepared to accept the

general views put forward during the discussion, but on the understanding that he was entitled to criticize or raise the personal issue of
the leadership within the NEC. This represented a withdrawal on his
part, as the point at issue was precisely Laski's resort to publishing
articles in order to criticize Labour leaders. His explanation was therefore accepted by 13 votes to 4, which indicated a considerable number
of abstentions. The following month he introduced a special motion
at the NEC, urging it to hold an early meeting with the Prime Minister
'with a view to discussing the direction of policy', but the committee
only agreed that the Labour cabinet ministers be asked to meet it.[41]

Just as the military reverses in the early part of the year had served
to strengthen the Left's overall critique of the war, so too did the military successes at the end of 1942 emasculate it. The moment of maximum political opportunity passed with the news of the initial British
victories in the North African desert. The Labour leadership had
weathered the storm. Bevan, typically, claimed that he had been
proved right; new weapons had been introduced (*ie*, Sherman tanks),
the high command had been changed (*ie*, Auchinleck removed), and
there had been better co-ordination between the air force and the
army.[42] Yet the most significant of the Left's campaigns – that for a
second front – had been lost. By January 1943, 'A Military Correspondent' in *Tribune* conceded that 'As far as France and the Low
Countries are concerned, the cost of an invasion would be out of all
proportion to the gain'.[43]

Laski's rhetorical appeal, in a New Year's Day message,[44] for the
Party to stand up for its principles, rang rather hollow. The Left was
in a state of political and intellectual disarray during most of the first
half of 1943. Bevan and Kingsley Martin were among those who
privately agreed in January that Cripps had now lost all influence in
the Commons.[45] Bevan himself, in March, reversed his former argument and declared that 'Labour Must Stay In The Government'. They
had not come so far only to see the reward of their sacrifices (on domestic issues) thrown away, but these were of lesser significance than
defeating the Nazis and taking some of the burden off the Soviet
Union.[46] As for Laski, he suffered a nervous breakdown in the summer.[47] In any case, Attlee and Bevan at first, and by October all the
Labour ministers, were in fact urging the cause of domestic reconstruction planning upon a reluctant Prime Minister.[48]

During the course of 1942, it was the very outcome of the war which had been uppermost in the minds of Labour's leaders. The basic premise of British strategy then decided was that, primarily, the war would be fought between the Russians and the Germans. It was only in 1943, after the battle of Kursk-Orel, when the initiative passed to the Russians, that British strategic thought seriously turned to the global or, at least, European consequences of an eventual Russian victory. Nevertheless, it had become apparent before then that Britain might have the possibility of exercising a strategic choice of great international significance and the Labour leaders were resolved that when such time came they would take a full part in the determination of British policy.

CHAPTER VII

Labour and the Politics of the War, 1941–43

LABOUR greeted Russia's entry into the war against Germany with a statement as curt as it was pointed. The NEC, the NCL and the general council of the TUC jointly expressed support for the efforts of the Soviet Union against Hitlerism but warned that there could be no question of any association with the British Communist Party.[1] Attlee's own, more general, views may be gathered from an exchange with Laski in December 1941. Laski had sent Attlee a proof copy of a pamphlet, 'Great Britain, Russia and the Labour Party', in which Laski contended that a reasonable post-war peace could be achieved only 'by a supreme effort both from the British Labour movement and from the Government of the Soviet Union'. This had led Laski into a 'Left understands Left' argument, though with the qualification that Russia would have to substitute 'co-operation for domination'. Attlee had not the slightest sympathy for this approach and was irritated by Laski's academic Marxism.[2] As well, the most influential figure in the TUC, Walter Citrine, had made his antipathy to Russian Communism clear in a remarkably frank interview with Eden, in August 1941. Feeling that some contact between the trade union movement and the Soviet Union was inevitable, Citrine wanted (in Eden's words) 'to control it and put his men in charge of it . . . You know Citrine's feelings about Communism,' (Eden added, in a note to Churchill) 'which he expressed again with undiminished emphasis, even going so far as to say that, were he given a choice between life under Nazi or Soviet rule, he would be in doubt as to which to choose.'[3]

Even Cripps, just prior to the German attack on Russia, had reached the conclusion that it might be better to wait for the growth of mutual trust between the United Kingdom and USSR over a period of military and economic co-operation before any attempt was made to define political relations in the form of a written agreement. Indeed, as Ambassador in Moscow, he had become so irritated by the difficulties in coming to a military arrangement that he told Churchill in June 1940 that the Soviet government either had to co-operate fully or the British should leave them alone.[4] The essence of the intellectual Left's ideological dilemma at the time of the war's most portentous development is perhaps best revealed in a book by G. D. H. Cole, published in September 1941. Since Germany had attacked Russia, he could now envisage only two possible endings to the war – a Nazi-dominated Europe or a Socialist Europe. Speculating about the latter, Cole suggested that there might be two, or even three, forms of 'Socialism', represented in several groupings such as a 'liberal' Western Socialist Europe, a Central Socialist Europe and an Eastern Soviet Socialist Europe. One bloc, however, would be best and Great Britain should be in it. But then came the dilemma. On the one hand Cole preferred to see an unchanged Soviet Union dominant over all Europe rather than an attempt 'to restore the pre-war States to their futile and uncertain independences and their petty economic nationalism under capitalist domination'. On the other, he personally had not 'the smallest intention of proposing, or of working for, the all-European victory of Communism à la Russe'. For he was not a Communist, but a West European liberal.[5]

Cripps, the man on the spot, was the first to react to the new situation. After a personal interview with Stalin in July he played a leading role in the negotiation of the Anglo-Soviet Agreement by which the two governments pledged mutual assistance to each other in the war and declared that no armistice or peace would be concluded with Hitlerite Germany, except by mutual arrangement. He also suggested the joint Anglo-Soviet military intervention in Iran, which took place in August and September, besides pressing hard for an increase in military assistance to the Russians.[6] By November, Cripps had become convinced of the necessity for a post-war settlement based on a wartime political accord between Great Britain, the USA and the USSR. The USSR had already, in September, subscribed to the Atlantic Charter. Cripps threatened to resign unless the government sent Eden, as well as the Chiefs of Staff, to Moscow in order to initiate political discussions.[7]

During this visit Stalin made it clear that, if Russia prevailed against Germany, she would insist on the British government's recognition of the Curzon line, of Russia's claim to the Baltic States, and of the transfer of East Prussia to Poland – that is to say, Russia's 1941 frontiers, except for Finland (where Stalin wanted those of 1940) and the transfer of East Prussia. Stalin also proposed immediate British recognition of these frontiers, which took even the Soviet Ambassador to Great Britain by surprise.[8] (Maisky knew that the British had promised Roosevelt not to re-arrange frontiers during the war.) But the British cabinet were unanimous at this juncture; no agreement on the basis of the USSR's proposals could be signed. This was a cabinet, it may be emphasized, from which both Churchill and Eden were absent – hence Labour opinion weighed very strongly indeed. Quite apart from the Atlantic Charter, and the promise to the United States, it was considered that a dangerous precedent would be created if a commitment in regard to territorial boundaries was entered into with one Ally. Inevitably they would be forced to enter into other such agreements with other Allies.[9]

It should be stressed, however, that for the Labour ministers as much as for Churchill,[10] the Atlantic Charter was not a document to be taken literally. It was to be regarded as an instrument of propaganda, and a diplomatic tool. Its main purpose was to increase American involvement in the war. Attlee took a leading part in the war cabinet's consideration of the draft version; the cabinet's suggestion of an additional paragraph about social security was accepted by Churchill and Roosevelt.[11] Although there was some hesitation on the part of the cabinet in regard to Clause Four – the intention 'to further the enjoyment by all States, great or small, victor or vanquished, on equal terms, to the trade and to the raw materials of the world which are needed for their economic prosperity' – this was overcome by the insertion of the prior qualifying phrase, 'with due respect for their existing obligations'.[12]

Shortly afterwards, Attlee indicated his particular satisfaction with the Charter, and its implications. Reporting to the war cabinet on his visit to Canada and the United States – which had taken place between October 25 and November 14, 1941, and during the course of which he had seen the President twice and every member of the United States cabinet – he remarked on the keen American interest in post-war problems. 'The Atlantic Charter has set out the principles upon which the Free Peoples intend to proceed,' he stated; it would not be wise to attempt to elaborate those principles in any public statement or document. 'Too much concentration on post-war problems,' he added frankly, 'affords an opportunity for those who will not face up to war to salve their consciences by planning a new world.' So much, it would seem, for some of his own Left-wingers! At the same time, he emphasized that the work of planning a new world could neither be postponed nor left to others. It was, Attlee thought,

> . . . most desirable that the American people should get accustomed to thinking of themselves as bound, through the facts of the situation, to take a big share of the responsibility for the post-war settlement and, as jointly concerned with us, to maintain the democratic way of life. The more they envisage the end, the more must they provide the means . . . [13]

The British Foreign Office was by no means as sanguine. In January 1942, the first of what became a long series of wide-ranging reappraisals of the European situation was prepared, which emphasized the need for post-war collaboration with Russia as the inevitable counter-weight to Germany. If a choice had to be made between Russia and the United States, the memorandum argued, then British interests would impel a choice of the latter. But, if possible, British policy should be directed towards the avoidance of such a choice. The aim, instead, should be to concert Anglo-Russian and Anglo-American policy. The urgent question was how to bring about an immediate improvement in Anglo-Soviet relations. What the Foreign Office suggested in January was that if the President was unable to agree to the Russian demands, then Britain (despite the Atlantic Charter) should propose Anglo-American support after the war either for the acquisition by the USSR of bases in contiguous territories, especially in the Baltic or Black Sea regions, or control by the Soviet government of the foreign policy and defence of the Baltic States. [14] Eden buttressed this suggestion at the end of January, pointing out to the cabinet that, if Hitler were defeated, it seemed certain that Russian forces would stand much further westward than in 1941, and that the Soviets would not accept, in victory, frontiers shallower than those across which they had been attacked in 1941. [15]

The cabinet was of several minds on the question. Beaverbrook not only urged that Stalin's request about frontier changes be accepted forthwith, but also that Britain recommend that the United States should accept it as well. [16] Eden proposed that the United States should be told that Britain wanted to accept Stalin's claims. But among the Labour cabinet ministers, only Morrison appears to have been favourably disposed towards them. Churchill referred to the uncertainty of the position at the end of the war; the matter should be left to the peace conference. He favoured a 'balanced presentation' to the United States. Bevin stated frankly the importance he attached to it being clearly understood whether Stalin's claim to his 1941 boundaries in Finland, the Baltic States and Bessarabia, represented Stalin's ultimate claims in this direction. Attlee declared that Eden's proposal was dangerous and might stultify the causes for which they were fighting. The action proposed was, for him, only too reminiscent of what had been done in the last war. Furthermore, as soon as one claim had been agreed to, they would be faced with others. . . . It implied that after the war they would be faced with the same old problems of strategic frontiers, and so forth. . . .[17]

Attlee's apparent ingenuousness lends itself to several interpretations, though one may be stressed. Writing to Churchill the following month, Beaverbrook mentioned that Attlee had threatened to resign if the 1941 frontiers were recognized. The threat was hardly serious – in fact 'no more than a passing exchange in the course of discussion'[18] according to Beaverbrook who had, in turn, threatened to resign if the 1941 frontiers were *not* recognized. Nevertheless, the underlying import is clear enough; Attlee yielded to no one in the cabinet in his fundamental – one might say ideological – suspicion of and antagonism towards Soviet Russia. During the cabinet contretemps with Beaverbrook early in 1942, Attlee – in Beaverbrook's eyes, became 'the symbol of opposition to a policy of friendship with the Soviet Union . . .'.[19] Bevin's position accorded with a line he had taken in January 1942 when lunching with Sikorski, the Polish leader. The latter, who had recently met Stalin, took the view that Russian successes had made Stalin more imperialistic in his demands. Sikorski informed Bevin that Stalin had offered the Poles the line of the River Oder as the post-war Polish-German frontier. To this Bevin, according to Dalton, replied that 'the Oder was too far West'.[20] Cripps, upon his return from Russia in January, adopted a similar view.[21]

Apart from Morrison,[22] the only other important Labour leader in government circles who took a favourable view of Russian policy was Dalton and his views were governed, in the first place, by his attitude to Germany. Dalton had been sent an almost verbatim report of Eden's talks with Stalin in December 1941 though, curiously enough, Eden had refused to send one to Morrison. On January 10, 1942, Dalton privately analysed this report. '. . . Stalin's remarks (with the exception of one point),' he wrote, 'showed both wisdom and common sense.' If Russia won the war she would, in any case, take physical control of the Baltic States and Finland. Stalin, Dalton believed, would agree to the United Kingdom being the dominant power in Western Europe, even a federated Western Europe, as long as Germany was broken up. It was the United States who would most probably object to Great Britain becoming predominant in post-war Western Europe, and a price might have to be paid. Britain, Dalton believed, would have to make a choice, either of being the political and economic centre of the British Empire, including the Dominions, or of leading a European bloc. Dalton favoured the second choice – the Dominions already showed signs of moving into the American orbit. He thought that 'a sensible deal, both with the Russians and the Americans', was not out of the question.[23]

At a meeting on February 6, 1942, the war cabinet advised the sending of a 'balanced statement' to the United States, setting out the reasons why it was desirable to go as far as possible to meet Stalin's claims – and also the objections to them![24] This somewhat artful tactic was a testimony to the magnitude and delicacy of the problem which was to be presented to British wartime diplomacy. Before the end of the month the cabinet had formally recognized that there was but one method whereby the aims of British European policy could be achieved – by tripartite discussion and agreement.[25] In the meantime, Soviet Russia had to be kept in play. Acting speedily on this recognition, Churchill wrote personally to Roosevelt on March 7, 1942, saying that 'the increasing gravity of the war has led me to feel that the principles of the Atlantic Charter ought not to be construed so as to deny Russia the frontiers she occupied when Germany attacked her'.[26]

Roosevelt had intimated that he wanted to handle the matter himself, which had not pleased the British war cabinet, apart from Churchill. In the first place, the cabinet ministers did not think Roosevelt appreciated the difficulties of reaching an agreement with Russia. Probably more important was the fact that they knew the President intended to strike a bargain with Russia over the Japanese War. As well, there was no liking for the idea of the United States taking the lead in the negotiations.[27] In any case, nothing had come from the Soviet-American exchanges and, by the end of March 1942, it was clear to the British that any further delay would be harmful. The Russians were anxious to negotiate and the cabinet was acutely aware that Britain could do very little to help Russia militarily – besides knowing full well the converse – that the Russian struggle against Germany was doing a great deal to help Britain militarily. The decision was made, therefore, to go ahead and negotiate unilaterally with the USSR on the basis of frontier claims. The issue for Russia, Eden noted in a cable to Halifax, was not merely one of security, but also of psychology – the question of confidence and equality with the Western Powers.[28] Yet the terms of the treaty that Britain concluded with the USSR, and indeed the whole episode, lend very little support to Sir Llewellyn Woodward's contention that, having to choose between giving way to either the Russians or the Americans, the cabinet decided to satisfy the Russians.[29] The overall object of British policy, as noted, was the avoidance of any such choice. Eden was basically successful in this respect, though if he actually 'satisfied' anyone, it was the Americans. Cadogan noted that John G. Winant, the American Ambassador, had been twisting Eden's tail.[30] Winant did likewise to Molotov, or at any rate told the Russian Foreign Minister that though there were certain dangers in proceeding with an Anglo-Russian Political Treaty at that time, the United States government had no objection to a Treaty of Mutual Assistance.[31]

Molotov had made it quite clear that what the Russians wanted was, firstly, an assurance about the second front and, secondly, a specific recognition of their frontier claims.[32] They received neither. Instead they were handed an *aide-mémoire* about the former, and eventually accepted the Treaty of Mutual Assistance in place of an agreement about the latter. It is true that the Treaty implied British support for some of Russia's proposed post-war changes in Eastern Europe but, as Eden informed the cabinet, specific negotiations broke down over 'the manner in which Poland's interests should be safeguarded under the Political Treaty in connection with her frontiers with the Soviet Union, and other matters'.[33] Russian acceptance of the Mutual Assistance Treaty was thus regarded as something in the nature of a diplomatic coup. The war cabinet was considerably relieved,[34] the Labour members, it may be surmised, as much as anyone. Eden himself was so impressed that he assured the cabinet of his conviction that Molotov was now anxious to co-operate with Britain after the war.[35] The Treaty was followed by some signs of improvement in Anglo-Soviet relations – until Churchill informed Stalin in Moscow in October that there would definitely be no second front that year. All future British plans for the post-war settlement of Europe hopefully anticipated American, as well as Russian, participation. To the Foreign Office it seemed that such plans

> ... had a logical and practical priority for the future of Germany. If the Great Powers remained united and if they set up a World Organization dominated by themselves, they could determine without much difficulty what should happen to a defeated Germany.[36]

An early 'Four-Power Plan' was sent to Churchill by the Foreign Office in October 1942. China was included to please the Americans, but the intention was that, effectively, it would be a Three-Power Plan, unless the admission of France to the post-war Great Power Club could be secured. As a method of obtaining Allied post-war collaboration the Plan was essentially negative, being directed 'against preventing German-Japanese aggression'.[37] Cripps was the only Labour minister to comment on this plan during the remainder of 1942. While expressing general agreement, he specifically proposed a Council of Europe (besides other regional Councils) to deal with political, economic and social issues (including minority issues) likely to disturb the peace. His Council of Europe would have had the United States, the USSR and Britain as members, and would have aimed at as much free trade as possible.[38] The war cabinet considered these ideas in November and though accepting generally the principle of Four-Power co-operation, came to no specific conclusions. Nor was the topic discussed again until just prior to Eden's visit to the United States in 1943. Bevin's ideas at the end of 1942 turned on the 'need for an economic basis for collective security', for which he suggested, in a memorandum to Eden, three possible frameworks, *viz.*, the United Nations, the European Commonwealth (beginning with the exiled governments and including Great Britain), and the British Commonwealth, including India and the Colonies.[39]

By the end of the year, with Russia continuing to hold out, the Labour ministers had become more wary of too obviously irritating the Soviet Union. The same was true of the majority of the cabinet, though not of Churchill. In December the cabinet met to consider the effect of the recent military successes in North Africa on Italy. The Prime Minister, in a cabinet note, had not been prepared to rule out the possibility of a separate peace; he did not think that it was necessarily in British interests that the Germans should have to occupy Italy.

Apprehension was expressed at the meeting about the political consequences of dealing with people who had been formerly associated with
Fascism.[40] The record does not specify this as a Labour opinion, but
in all likelihood it was, in view of what happened the following
month. For the moment the cabinet was content to agree that its hands
should not be tied in any way regarding the type of Italian government
with which Britain would be prepared to negotiate a separate peace.
It stipulated, however, that the United States and the USSR be
informed of the recent inquiries which had been made by individual
Italians. And when, in January 1943, the issue of 'unconditional surrender' first arose, somewhat unexpectedly, at the Casablanca Conference, the cabinet's response to a cable from Churchill was
unanimous. The Prime Minister had asked about the unconditional
surrender of Germany and Japan, specifically excluding Italy in the
hope of encouraging a political break-up there. The war cabinet
without exception considered that the balance of advantage lay against
excluding Italy because of the 'misgivings' which would inevitably
be aroused in Turkey, the Balkans and elsewhere. Generally, the war
cabinet thought that it would be a mistake, at any rate at that stage, to
make any distinction between the three partners in the Axis.[41] The
continuing uncertainties of the military situation, coupled with the
ambiguities of the wartime alliance at that point, necessitated the
acceptance of the 'unconditional surrender' policy. The Labour ministers must have considered that the latter was the minimum of diplomatic cement required to guarantee the survival of the alliance (in the
absence of specific war aims) to the successful end of the German war,
to say nothing of the future. Their general outlook had not changed –
on the contrary; but if the year had brought an increased realization
of their antipathy to both Nazi Germany and Soviet Russia, it had
also revealed something of the potential international political com-
plexities.

Certain Labour tendencies, however, had become evident before
1943. Determined as they were to see the war against Germany brought
to a militarily successful and politically decisive conclusion, the Labour
leaders were well aware of the implications this held for the future
position of Russia in Europe. They did not like these implications and
they intended to do all they could to limit them, at the appropriate
time. American involvement in the European settlement appeared to
be the best possible way of achieving this, preferably during the war

itself. Yet the assumptions involved in the creation of a world organization dominated by the Great Powers were very large, and Attlee and Bevin in particular were not overly impressed by such schemes. They were, consequently, to play a most active role in the formulation of a British insurance policy – both in regard to Germany itself and also in regard to the possibility that Russia might not 'co-operate' in a European settlement. For the time being, the imperative need was to keep the Russians in play and, especially, to avoid giving them needless grounds for suspicion. The Labour ministers had thus acted to check Churchill's impetuosity in connection with Italy. The episode marked the beginning of Labour's direct participation in the method as well as the substance of British wartime foreign policy making.

CHAPTER VIII

The Labour Ministers and British Re-appraisals of European Policy in 1943

DURING the course of 1943 the problem of Germany's future – and also that of Europe's – assumed a new, more practical character because, from about the middle of the year the Russians went over to the offensive. Militarily, this marked the turning-point of the war. Though Germany was far from beaten, it was increasingly apparent that the end of her second bid to dominate Europe was only a matter of time. Hitherto, international politics had been largely left to the battlefield, the Russian battlefield so far as Europe directly was concerned. Henceforth, the committee-room and the conference-table should have been – from the British point of view – equally the focal points for decision. Here the British intended to take a larger part; and here also the Labour ministers were to be given a full opportunity of relating personal conviction to realistic possibility.

Before the wartime negotiations were concluded at Potsdam, the Labour ministers were 'playing the British hand' (as Churchill might have expressed it) alone. Yet a perceptible increase in the influence and activity of the Labour cabinet ministers in the field of foreign affairs is evident long before that. In fact, at no time in the existence of the Coalition government was Labour's voice more pronounced than during the last two years. *Prima facie*, the continuation of the Coalition until the end of the war is itself the most obvious indication of Labour's official responsibility for such policy as emerged, but it is possible to be more specific. Nominally, Labour possessed only three out of ten seats in the war cabinet, those of Attlee, Bevin and Morrison. But, this was not only a politically powerful trio; R. G. Casey, the Australian diplomat, was Minister Resident in the Middle East; Halifax continued as Ambassador in Washington, and Lord Woolton did not join the war cabinet until November 1943. Therefore, when Churchill and Eden consulted the cabinet from abroad, they were in fact consulting with the three Labour ministers plus Sir John Anderson, Oliver Lyttelton and, after November 1943, Woolton. None of the latter were of the same political stature as the Labour men at that time. Anderson, perhaps the most imposing figure personally, was not formally attached to any political party. More important, Attlee and Bevin possessed the psychological advantage of being, with Churchill, the longest serving – and virtually irremovable – members of the war cabinet. This was to be reflected in the vigour of their contributions.

Attlee was not a man who changed either his political views or his ideological antipathies easily. He warned Dalton at the beginning of the year that after the war the Russians would possibly want to absorb all the Slav States. Dalton agreed that this might be so, although Stalin had expressly disclaimed such intentions. Dalton added that he would not like to see the Russians try to absorb Germany as a Soviet socialist republic, as they might find Germany running Russia as well as Germany! Attlee refrained from making any comment, but that they must make no mistake this time in rendering Germany unable to repeat her aggressions. They had been too tender to her last time, though he had not thought so then.[1] This view in no way affected Attlee's attitude towards Russia. When, in May, Churchill heard about Stalin's abolition of the Comintern, he immediately cabled from Washington asking Attlee for the war cabinet's reaction. The Prime Minister was especially anxious to have the opinion of the Labour ministers, for though, at first sight, Churchill thought the news was 'very fine', he wondered if there might be a snag. In any case, he wanted to send Stalin a telegram. Attlee's instant reply was that the cabinet unanimously considered that it would be a mistake to send a telegram or to make any public comment.[2] Churchill's Labour colleagues were agreed that indeed there might be a snag.

There was a further dimension to the preliminary British discussions of post-war policy in 1943, that of the Imperial or Commonwealth connection. Attlee communicated his views regarding this subject to his cabinet colleagues on June 15. 'I take it to be a fundamental assumption,' he wrote,

that whatever post-war international organization is established, it will be our aim to maintain the British Commonwealth as an international entity, recognized as such by foreign countries, in particular by the U.S. and the Soviet Union. If we are to carry our full weight in the post-war world with the U.S. and the U.S.S.R., it can only be as a united British Commonwealth.

He added that it would be necessary to satisfy the legitimate claim of each of the Dominions to rank in the world as an independent nation, and he suggested that the most practical course was to have the United Kingdom and one Dominion represented on the various international committees that would be established.[3]

After Roosevelt's public sponsorship of the 'unconditional surrender' policy, at the beginning of 1943 coupled with the Darlan incident,* it had become evident that the British needed a more intimate assessment of American opinion. Before leaving for Washington in March, Eden circulated a paper on Germany which outlined several possible policies, of which the single aim would be the disarmament of Germany and the prevention of her rearmament. While the paper was not conclusive as regards either the frontier question or the type of future German government, the Foreign Office accepted the implication of 'unconditional surrender'; there would have to be a 'total military occupation of Germany'. But, in Washington, Eden – and thus the cabinet – were given plenty of food for thought. American thinking seemed to favour a joint Allied occupation of Germany, in order to avoid a division resulting in spheres of influence. The President, Eden was informed, saw no difficulty on the Polish question. Dismemberment would be the only safe solution of the German problem. Furthermore, the Russian claim to the Baltic States was now acceptable to the United States, and the Americans took the view that 'even if the Russians were aiming at extending their influence over Europe, our attempt to work with them would not make matters any worse'.[4] The tone of these remarks was hardly calculated to reassure the British, but there was another American view – that of Sumner Welles, the influential Under-Secretary of State – and it was this that Eden per-

---

* Darlan was an Anglophobe French admiral who became one of the most important advocates of Vichy collaboration with the Nazis. By accident he happened to be in North Africa when the Allies invaded on November 8, 1942. At first Darlan was prepared to resist but after Hitler occupied the whole of southern France, on November 11, he threw in his lot with the Americans. A cease-fire followed throughout Algeria and Morocco and Darlan was allowed to retain his authority. This provoked a storm of protest in Britain. Churchill was obliged to explain to the Commons in secret session that the deal was a temporary expedient to save bloodshed. Darlan's assassination, on November 24, came as a political relief which did not, however, remove Left-wing Labour forebodings.

sonally related to the Cabinet on his return. Welles, Eden stated, a keen advocate of dismemberment, had included as part of his plan a proposal that

> ... for the purposes of our military occupation of Germany immediately after the war, we should make military divisions (with separate Commands, etc.) corresponding broadly to the areas of separate States into which we hoped the Greater Germany would be broken up.

Eden stressed that he regarded the last point as a new and valuable contribution.[5] During the course of the year, Attlee came largely to agree with him.

On his trip to the United States in May, the main purpose of which was to persuade the Americans to agree to an extension of the Mediterranean strategy, the Prime Minister contented himself with airing his views to a number of important American figures, though not to the President, about a world council, regional councils, a strong France, the detachment of Prussia from Germany, and the association of the USA in the policing of Europe.[6] Probably in deference to the President's strong views on the subject, Churchill felt obliged to cable to the war cabinet that urgent consideration should be given to the question of the elimination of de Gaulle as a political force. The cabinet's response was an unequivocal negative – with Attlee, Bevin and Morrison in particular taking this view.[7]

When the cabinet met to consider the question of Germany, in June 1943, it was still reluctant to commit itself. Two memoranda were presented, one by Eden[8] and the other by Cripps.[9] Eden formally proposed that for the purpose of occupation Germany should be divided into three zones, principally British, Russian and American, but which would include forces from the smaller Allies under inter-Allied command. This, according to Eden, would maintain the principle of a joint United Nations' occupation, but the problem of supply and administration would thereby be simplified. No one, however, could have been under any illusion as to what might develop, if only because Cripps, in his memorandum, emphasized what might be involved. He agreed with that American view, he stated adroitly, which argued that a three-way division of Germany would lead directly to spheres of influence. Cripps advanced three reasons for a 'mixed' form of United Nations' administration throughout the occupied territories; zones of influence were not conducive to Big Three harmony, the enforcement of a unitary policy would be difficult, and the success of the United Nations idea itself would depend upon the development of habits of co-operation. Several ministers expressed agreement with Cripps's memorandum but others, on the other hand, stressed the grave administrative difficulties. The cabinet decided that more consideration of both points of view was required.[10]

In July, Attlee submitted two papers to the cabinet, one dealing specifically with Germany,[11] the other with the broader aspect of the post-war international situation.[12] In the former he noted that, though everyone was agreed that there could be no dealing with the Nazis, he had observed 'a tendency to think that we would have to treat with some kind of German authority without specifying what this should or should not be'. Attlee was concerned lest there should be a repetition of what had happened after the last war when, in his opinion, first the Kaiser had been made the scapegoat for Germany, and then the democratic parties had been made the scapegoat for Versailles, while 'all the time the real aggressive elements' had been left untouched. He was referring primarily to the Prussian Junker class, with its strong roots in the Reichswehr and the Civil Service, allied to the masters of heavy industry. As well, there had been added South German elements, especially in Bavaria. How far these had used the Nazis, or had been used by them, might be open to debate, but it was not out of the question that they might liquidate Hitler and his gang, and come forward as the only body which could save central Europe from anarchy. Last time these forces had maintained themselves because of the Allies' fear of Bolshevism. Attlee insisted that this must not happen again. The Prussian virus had to be eradicated, and there was no reason why the big industrial combines should be allowed to continue.

It could be that the Russians, Czechs and Poles would liquidate the Junkers, or even that the Germans themselves would deal with some of the aggressive elements, the Labour leader speculated. But, in addition, Attlee was emphatic that 'very positive action will have to be taken by the victorious Powers if there is to be a new orientation of the German nation'. Neither the encouragement of particularist tendencies, nor a *cordon sanitaire*, or the prohibition of aircraft, or aircraft factories would suffice. The German industries should be controlled in the interests of Europe and operated in the interests of Central and South-Eastern Europe, though German workers could be permitted good conditions. German officials, however, could not be left in control. Clearly, Attlee favoured substantial changes inside Germany, not merely in respect of Nazism. Indeed, what he seems to have wanted was not far short of the type of 'revolution' advocated by his own Left wing, as far as Germany was concerned.

In his second paper, Attlee indicated his broad agreement with Churchill's outline of the post-war political machinery, and also with the significance that Eden attached to United States approval of any such scheme. Regarding the European settlement, Attlee pointed out that British policy had long been influenced by the dual position of the British Isles, lying on the fringe of Europe and, at the same time, being the heart of a world empire. They had tried to ensure that continental commitments would not be such as to prevent throwing a sufficient force behind any part of the overseas Empire which might be threatened. The ideal had been a state of equilibrium in Europe which left British military forces free to meet contingencies overseas. Now, Attlee warned, they might have to recognize that no equilibrium in Europe was likely to be obtainable for a long time to come. If they had to undertake continental commitments for an indefinite period, it would mean 'banking on the chance that no major attempt [would] be made outside Europe to upset the world settlement until the state of affairs in Europe permitted us to withdraw or disperse our forces'. At the same time, particularly in an age of air-power, they could not afford to take risks in Europe. ... The key to this riddle, in Attlee's opinion, was the United States. If the Americans would provide forces for Europe, the Dominions would agree to any settlement there on which Britain and the United States were agreed. If, however, the United States would not provide forces, then the British would have to let America exclusively look after the East. This would disrupt the Commonwealth, weaken the Dominions and increase the risk of Big Power rivalry. Attlee concluded that

> ... in the interests of the solidarity of the British Commonwealth we should hesitate again to enter, *without the U.S.* [Attlee's emphasis], into any military guarantees of the Locarno type, *ie*, a continental obligation, not shared by the Dominions ...

What Attlee was saying may be more succinctly expressed as follows— Germany had to undergo a thorough social, political and economic change, but this would result in a power vacuum in Europe. Russia would predominate unless the British committed themselves to re-dressing the balance. If the British did this, the Empire would be endangered by American ambitions. The choice was between a balanced Europe and an Empire and, in this case, Attlee preferred to opt for the Empire, particularly in an age of air-power which left the homeland vulnerable. The only solution was that the Americans could be persuaded, or would volunteer, to provide forces for Europe. In that case, a balance of power could be obtained there and, at the same time, the Imperial or Commonwealth connection would be main-tained. It is hardly surprising that, having delivered himself of such views, Attlee found himself, in very short order, chairman of the three sub-committees of the war cabinet which dealt with the formulation of British post-war policy.

The first of these, an ad hoc committee on Armistice Terms, only met once, but from it the other bodies emerged. A meeting on July 21, attended by Eden and Sir James Grigg, the Secretary of State for War, and certain officials, dealt with Italy. A memorandum from Eden argued that while the USSR had, by agreement, to be a party to any arrangement by which hostilities with Italy were terminated, it was 'only natural' that Italy should be considered an Anglo-American theatre. The difficulty was that, if after Britain and the United States had considered the question bilaterally, the Soviets were not 'brought in', there was a risk that the Soviet government would act unilaterally in regard to Finland, Roumania and Hungary. Indeed, if by some chance Germany were to collapse as a result of Russian action in the field, Russia might even feel justified in acting unilaterally there. During the committee's discussion of this paper, someone – the record, unfortunately, does not disclose who – made the frank point that:

> Our object should be to keep as free a hand as possible, while at the same time avoiding laying ourselves open to a charge of breaking an agreement with the Russians, or giving them a pretext for failing to consult us in similar cases in future.

Attlee's sole recorded remark was to draw attention to a paragraph in the draft proclamation to the Italian people, and to suggest that it gave the impression that the Fascists might be left in power. He was in-formed that another wording, preferably drawn from the directive for the military government in Sicily, would be recommended instead. Negotiations on this were pending in Washington.

The committee's decision was to draw rather a fine distinction along the line taken by Eden's memorandum; the Russians would have to be consulted about the general terms to be imposed on a defeated Italy, but not about the particular Italian authority with whom a surrender agreement should be signed, nor about the details of such an agreement.[13] The reason for this decision, and Eden's memorandum, was evidently the Imperial connection, to which Attlee was firmly committed. Nevertheless, as an augury of future British negotiations with Russia it hardly boded well. Stalin, in fact, soon protested, declaring that all questions concerning the surrender of Italy should be considered by a politico-military commision of the three Allies. In the absence of the Prime Minister and the Foreign Secretary, who were both in Quebec, the war cabinet decided, on August 25, 1943, to recommend the acceptance of Stalin's proposal to the President and Prime Minister.[14] But, five days later, with Eden present, it was pointed out that previously Stalin had not known the full text of the Instrument of Surrender for Italy. This had now been communicated to him, and he had agreed to it. Thus the situation had altered; it was difficult to see what functions could be carried out by the commission if it were established in Sicily. At the same time, the war cabinet felt that though Stalin's proposal was not altogether appropriate in its present form, any suggestion which might seem to show reluctance towards it must be avoided at all costs. Yet the matter had to be handled in such a way that the proposed commission, once established, could be developed into a body on the lines the British had in mind.[15] The delicacy of the diplomatic task now confronting the British in regard to Russia may be underlined by reference to a further decision of the war cabinet in the autumn. Then, the entire war cabinet agreed with Churchill's stand against withdrawal of war material (especially landing-craft) from Italy at that time, even if it were to mean a delay of two or three months in the start of Overlord,[16] the code name used with reference to the proposed invasion of France. Such a delay at that time of the year would mean postponing the invasion until 1944, which would be certain to increase Russian suspicions. The diplomatic situation was further complicated by the fact that the Americans were already withdrawing landing-craft, if not planes. Nevertheless, the cabinet again endorsed Churchill's representations to the Americans not to withdraw Overlord material from the Mediterranean until after the conclusion of the Italian operation in November.[17]

Attlee continued to take a major part in the development of British policy towards Italy as the ad hoc committee was followed, in August 1943, by a ministerial committee on Armistice Terms and Civil Administration, of which he again was chairman. This body spent most of its time in the remainder of the year discussing Italian policy, but until the question of Anglo-American co-ordination (which proved very difficult) had been worked out, it was almost impossible for the British to arrive at any definite decisions. The political importance of this second committee, however, increased considerably from November 1943, as will be seen.

The third committee concerned with the post-war settlement, of which Attlee became chairman in the summer of 1943, was the war cabinet committee on the Post-War Settlement. Cripps was also appointed to this body, as was the Labour MP, George Tomlinson, the joint-parliamentary secretary to the Minister of Labour. The committee held its first meeting on August 5, and met three more times that month, after which it ceased to function, consideration of policy reverting directly to the war cabinet. From the start, the Post-War Settlement committee was confronted with a substantial volume of material, including the two papers by Attlee mentioned previously, and memoranda by both Cripps and Tomlinson. Cripps's paper, which concerned the relationship of the 'Proposed World Economic Organizations to the World Council', included a suggestion that the smaller countries should have more say in a World Economic Council than they would have in a World Political Council. Tomlinson, who was Bevin's nominee, stressed the importance of the International Labour Organization in relation to the same subject as Cripps. Eden also submitted a paper, and it was to this that the committee first addressed itself, at its second meeting on August 11, no doubt because Eden's paper was on 'The Future of Germany'.

The Foreign Secretary declared that he was not altogether satisfied with his own paper, but presumably this applied more especially to the first section of it, which was in the form of a general discussion of the political situation in Germany and included some speculation as to what sort of situation might or might not emerge. The second section formally proposed a total occupation of the country, in order to encourage decentralization. It was this last section which was new. Here a specific set of measures were advocated as being strategically necessary, politically expedient and economically desirable – provided that the victorious Powers retained in the post-war period a preponderance of armed strength, and the will to use it if necessary. These measures did not preclude – indeed were aimed – at the ultimate re-admission of Germany on an equal footing to the community of Europe. The proposed measures involved:

(a) Restoration of a free and independent Austria, possibly connected with some central European confederation.
(b) Restoration of Czechoslovakia.
(c) Restoration of pre-war territorial status in the Low Countries and Luxembourg.
(d) Restoration of Alsace-Lorraine to France.
(e) Cession to Poland of East Prussia, Danzig and the Oppeln district of Silesia.
(f) The transfer (if desired) of control of the Kiel Canal to the United Nations.
(g) The imposition of some form of international control on German industry and economic life.
(h) Encouragement of particularist and separatist movements, if they appeared, and the possible development of a federal Germany.[18]

In so far as they applied to boundaries, these objectives were generally acceptable to the committee. They were, indeed, not very far removed from those previously envisaged by Dalton, apart from the transfer of the Saar to France. But as a response to the question 'What sort of Germany?' Eden's proposals were found inadequate. The suggestion was made that, presumably, there were forces inside Germany that the British wished to encourage, and that these should be taken into account when framing policy. Though not identified as such, this is fairly easily recognizable as a Labour view. German economic and industrial matters were subsequently discussed, but no conclusions were recorded at the meeting, other than the call for reports by officials, and nothing of substance emerged from the committee's other meetings. Hence no report was made to the full war cabinet.

Here, too, British policy depended on inter-Allied agreement – preferably prior to the end of the war. The longer the war lasted, the more obvious British military weakness, both actual and potential – relative to the super-powers, became. From the middle of 1943 onwards it was apparent that time was not on Britain's side. 'If nothing was settled,' wrote Eden in retrospect, 'Soviet Russia would gain, because the chances were that her troops would be the first to reach German territory.'[19] Nor was this the only contingency, as Eden's lieutenant, William (later Lord) Strang, has indicated. When, in 1944, the European Advisory Commission (the EAC) was deliberating, the British negotiators also feared '. . . a Soviet decision *not* to cross the German frontier'.[20] Indeed, as late as January 1945, after the German counter-attack in the Ardennes, Churchill was anxiously cabling Stalin for reassurance about the Soviet drive westwards, and was delighted with the reply that the Soviets would try to speed it up.[21]

The results of the Moscow Foreign Ministers meeting held in October were somewhat deceptive, at least to the British. Both Eden, publicly,[22] and Churchill, privately,[23] were enthusiastic at the time about a conference which had established an advisory council for Italy, and the EAC, and which had issued the Four-Power Declaration. The fact of the matter, so far as the post-war political settlement in Europe was concerned, was that neither the Americans nor the Russians were now in as much of a hurry as the British. Agreeable as the tripartite meetings in 1943 had been in some respects, nothing had really been settled about Europe's future (except that the Nazi Party would have no share in it). Although Eden's proposal at Moscow for a 'European Advisory Commission to consider and make joint recommendations on European problems connected with the termination of hostilities' had been accepted without difficulty,[24] this clearly applied to the short-term. His original suggestion – that the EAC should deal with any European problem connected with the war, apart from military matters – was rejected by both Cordell Hull, the American Secretary of State, and Molotov.[25] And although each of the Foreign Ministers indicated that some measure of German dismemberment was desirable, the future of Germany had been neither seriously nor fully discussed.

It was in these circumstances that, towards the end of December 1943, Attlee's Armistice Terms and Civil Administration committee came to consider certain fresh proposals laid before it by the chiefs of staff. The committee, it should be noted, had been given in November a revised composition and wider terms of reference. These had been recommended to the war cabinet in a memorandum written by Attlee and approved by the cabinet at a meeting presided over by Attlee.[26] At the same meeting, Bevin had asked that he should be included on the ministerial Committee on Supply Questions in Liberated and Conquered Areas. The chiefs of staff's proposals took the form of a report,[27] which rested upon a number of minimal political assumptions. These were that the war against Japan would continue for some time after the defeat of Germany; that some kind of central administration would exist in Germany – though not necessarily a central government – as well as local authorities; that the bulk of the occupying forces – for a considerable time at any rate – would be supplied by Britain, the USA and the USSR, presumably in equal numbers; that bordering countries were to contribute token forces at first and more later; that Austria would not form part of Germany; that East Prussia, Danzig, and possibly other areas, would ultimately be given to Poland; that 'it will be the policy to confine Germany elsewhere within frontiers no wider than those which existed in 1937'; and that, if a zoning plan were agreed to, the boundaries of the zones were to be agreed before hostilities ceased and would consequently not depend on the positions which the forces of the three principal Allies respectively might have reached before the fighting stopped. Then, in more military fashion, the chiefs of staff set out what they considered to be the arguments for and against a total occupation of Germany. The conclusion was that it was essential if Germany was to be effectively disarmed, and 'its military spirit broken'. No one on the committee had any objection to this, perhaps least of all the Labour chairman, whose earlier suggestions had thus been given more definite shape.

The report expressed the hope that, after the problem of internal disorder had been overcome and the destruction of arms industries completed, the work of the Control Commission might be enforced mainly by a strong air force. But that was for the indefinite future. In the meantime, the chiefs of staff were clear that there should be three zones of occupation, plus a combined Berlin zone, and that in each zone forces from one Power should predominate. The crux of the report – and its new element – was the recommendation that Britain should occupy the north-western part of Germany, Russia the eastern part, and the United States southern Germany. As a wag was later supposed to have remarked, the British were to get the industry, the Russians the agriculture, and the Americans the scenery. The recommendation reflected both a deep antipathy towards Germany and a rock-bottom British view of post-war political realities, for there can be little doubt that it was designed – among other things – to insure against the possibility that the 'short-term' policy might have to become the basis of a long-term one. British occupation of the north-west zone represented a triple insurance – against a German resurgence, an American withdrawal and a predominant Russia. Attlee's committee lost no time in agreeing with the chiefs of staff and invited Eden to forward the report to William Strang on the EAC.[28] Moreover, though it was not accomplished without a long and hard struggle in the EAC, and later at Quebec, principally with the Americans, the British proposals were subsequently accepted by the other Allies, almost in their entirety. The political lesson of the year for the Labour ministers had been an old one; long-term goals usually have to be tempered with short-term practicalities.

CHAPTER IX

A Socialist Foreign Policy?

WHILE the Labour leaders were actively involved in the framing of British foreign policy in 1943, the Party as a whole was busy providing support for the proposition that a 'Socialist' or 'Labour' outlook in general does not necessarily lend itself to the advocacy of any particular foreign policy. The formulation of a coherent public Party pronouncement on the international post-war settlement was rendered virtually impossible by the varied, and often conflicting, ideas and attitudes that existed within the Party. Chief among these was probably the popular anti-German sentiment, but this produced its own reaction not confined to the group led by Stokes, or the Left wing. The latter, though somewhat subdued for the first half of the year, effected something like a resurgence afterwards – which is not to say that the Left was altogether agreed in its views; it was not. The leadership had somehow to contrive to accommodate these disparate elements, while at the same time leaving its own freedom of decision unimpaired. The net result was a confused Party 'ideologically', though it must be emphasized that the external situation itself was, indeed, perplexing.

The only specific reference to the peace in the NEC's report for 1942–43 was that its maintenance by 'the four most powerful United Nations – the British Commonwealth, America, Russia and China – should lead on to the establishment of a World Political Authority ...'. Otherwise, apart from the uncontroversial statement that the Axis Powers were to be disarmed, the delegates to the Party's annual conference in June were reminded of what they already knew – namely that 'Throughout the present War, the Labour Party has regarded, and still regards the winning of complete victory as its supreme aim'. Certainly, the conflict was one of 'principles', and preparation for necessary social change was an essential part of winning it. In fact, civilization would not escape another such disaster unless the war 'resulted in victory for our Socialist and Internationalist Cause'.[1] But passions ran high and were stilled neither by the 1943 report nor by the formal statement on the International Post-War Settlement the following year.

This situation was inherent in the nature and structure of the Party; criticism both of policy and leadership was permitted to a remarkable extent. In addition, there was an inevitable cleavage between those members who were privy to official (*ie*, governmental) information and decisions and those who were on the outside. But there was now no question of any real political threat to the Labour leadership. Characteristically, Bevan attempted to turn these points to his own advantage in August 1943; he stressed the difficulties under which the critics laboured. If the government listened to them and was subsequently successful, the government took the credit; if the government did not listen and failed, then everyone, including the critics, was involved in the failure. Acknowledging the government's strength, which was due to the military successes, he emphasized the point that military policy was one thing, the considerations which lay behind that policy another.[2] The fact remained that criticism – in the absence of specific indications of the government's intentions – was extremely difficult. It was obliged to focus on the lack of policy statements, or on personalities, as much as on government policy itself. Moreover, because the critics were often divided among themselves, the problem of leadership was made that much easier. In the end, the critics simply played into the hands of as subtle a political operator as Dalton.

The Left, it has been noted, tended to be on the defensive about the key issue, Germany, during the first half of 1943. Hence it was the maverick Stokes who first denounced the 'Unconditional Surrender' policy which he described in February as a negation of the Atlantic Charter and contrary to official Labour policy.[3] The *New Statesman* was considerably more circumspect, preferring at that stage to ask questions rather than to attempt any dogmatic response.[4] *Tribune* did not so much as mention the 'policy' until May, by which time the Left had regained some of its former assertiveness. Then, the paper felt able to describe it as '. . . a battle-cry necessary to convince the Russians of our good intentions, a slogan, a war-whoop . . .' and quite meaningless in practice.[5] By this time the question of German policy had produced some curious contortions in the Party at large. Kingsley Martin had no difficulty in condemning the lack of an 'escape clause' in the 'offer' to the Axis countries – but he did so in the course of some remarks approving the RAF's new 'precision attacks on dams and power stations followed by devastating raids on already disorganized and flooded towns'. He rejected the arguments of those who considered that the raids would not encourage the Germans to revolt.[6] H. G. Wells confessed that his former confidence in Vansittart had now evaporated.[7] Evidence that Gillies's views were not all-persuasive at Labour Party headquarters was provided by the issuing of a pamphlet on the subject of *The Other Germany* from Transport House. The pamphlet, written on behalf of 'The Executive Committee of the Trade Union Centre for German Workers in Great Britain', bluntly declared that condemnation of an entire people amounted to a counterpart of the Nazi *Herrenvolk* theory.[8]

Understandably, the tactic of the NEC for the 1943 annual conference was to continue avoiding any situation in which the emotional division in the Party could formally manifest itself. This was decided in May by a large majority of the executive. But the following month, less than two weeks before the scheduled opening of the conference, the NEC was obliged to consider the question again. Stokes had put forward a resolution directly challenging the 'Fight For Freedom' group who, in turn, were more than willing to accept a challenge. The NEC again decided, by 10 votes to 7, that 'it would be best to get this whole discussion called off'. Dalton voted with the majority, despite the fact that privately he viewed the Stokes resolution as 'declaring generally that Germans are good chaps and that no one should hate them'. That the NEC's effort was not entirely successful was due not only, as Dalton considered, to the 'stupidity and misdirected pugnacity of Stokes and Co.',[9] but equally to the determination of those who took the opposite view to influence official policy.

The conference's chairman, A. J. Dobbs, lost no time in raising the issue. He did not doubt, he informed the delegates in his opening address, that there were many people in Germany who had been opposed to Nazism in the early days of Hitler's power, or even that some Nazi opponents still remained. The point was, however, that they were 'quite ineffectual as an opposition' and therefore they should be prepared 'to agree with the conditions laid down by the United Nations, including . . . unilateral disarmament and Allied occupation for as long as is necessary to secure the re-education of the Nazified youth of Germany'. This was almost deliberately calculated to arouse the hackles of the Left, as well as those of Stokes's group. But Dobbs was still more provocative. Besides calling for the destruction of Junker militarist power and control of German industries 'actual and potential', he issued a specific warning about the danger of being 'too tolerant' after the war. Germans would remain Germans, not only responsible for Nazism but innately militaristic. The conflict came to a head in a debate on the Post-War Treatment of Enemy Peoples – a debate which resulted in an outright victory for the 'Fight For Freedom' supporters. It was a victory obtained in defiance of the executive, which considered that no pronouncement on the topic was possible or desirable at that juncture. Instead, the NEC promised that a statement would be made for a subsequent conference to accept or reject. Though a large number of delegates accepted this promise and abstained from voting on the issue, many others were provoked by the debate into doing so. A 'hard-line' policy was supported by some 1,800,000 votes to 700,000.[10]

The vote precipitated a flurry of Party activity after the conference, notably on the Left,[11] which did not prevent the 'hard-liners' from attempting to press home their tactical advantage. In August 1943, Gillies drew up a 'Draft Circular' for the 'guidance' of the NEC.[12] This Circular underlined the fact that the Party, in effect, had condemned the German people as a whole. It purported to review the steps by which the Party had been inevitably brought to this position, repugnant as it was to traditional thought and practice. The intention behind the Circular was to make it as difficult as possible for the NEC to modify the conference's decision. Gillies despatched a slightly revised version of the original document to all members of the executive in September, together with some adverse comments from Laski.

Unfortunately for Gillies, the TUC's annual conference took place before the NEC was called upon to come to any decision. Charles Dukes, of the General and Municipal Workers Union, introduced a resolution in the debate on the Treatment of Post-War Germany along practically identical lines to the one which had been carried at the Party conference, but the result was the reverse of what had happened on that occasion. In spite of vociferous support from a trade-union MP, F. Marshall, Dukes's resolution was overwhelmingly defeated in favour of an amendment which specifically distinguished between the Nazis and Germans in general.[13] Either the discussion subsequent to the Party conference had had some effect or some of the trade-union leaders had had their own, considerable, second thoughts. At any rate, the effect of the amendment carried at the TUC meeting was also to delete passages from the original resolution calling for the unilateral disarmament, long-term occupation and re-education of Germany.

The absurdity of the situation did not go unnoticed by the Party's hierarchy. Noel-Baker wrote directly to Attlee about the episode, urging him to intervene.[14] Attlee, sensitive as always to the question of Party unity, did intervene; when Gillies's Circular came before the NEC's International sub-committee it was rejected. As well, the sub-committee resolved to have no further papers on the treatment of enemy peoples for the time being.[15] This did not go far enough for Noel-Baker, who called Attlee's attention to two other matters which, in Noel-Baker's opinion, were related: one was that of the Party's general attitude to the Social Democratic parties of all the enemy countries; the other concerned the elimination of Gillies and the composition of the sub-committee itself.[16] Attlee, however, had not changed his mind about Germany; the German Social Democrats were not permitted to address or attend subsequent Labour Party conferences during the war. Moreover, however maladroit Attlee might have thought Gillies, the latter remained at his post until March 8, 1945. Above all, the matter now reverted to the 'anti-German' hands of Dalton.[17]

The intensity of the emotions aroused within Labour circles over the issue of Germany undoubtedly left its mark upon the atmosphere in which other aspects of European peace-making were discussed. Issues tended to be over-simplified, particularly as the 'soft-liners', on the whole, were on the Left wing and took a more optimistic view of the possibility of amicable post-war relations with the Soviet Union. By the same token, those who favoured a more punitive peace with Germany tended to be altogether more dogmatically anti-Communist in ideological outlook and therefore more cautious about and suspicious of Russian motives. Policy-making might well have been easier if it had been the other way round! But, in any case, the actual situation was far more complicated than that for, as noted previously, Stokes was certainly anti-Communist, whereas Dalton, who strove to play down ideological attitudes generally, thought there were reasons why a compromise with Russia in Europe might be worked out. Except in regard to German policy Labour's official attitude to international affairs generally in the last years of the war tended to become more and more open-ended. Such pragmatism, especially on the part of the old leadership, was usually couched in the emotive language of pre-war years, but not so much because of any deliberate intention to mislead as because the leadership still thought in such terms.

This did not apply to Dalton, who took considerable pride, it will have been observed, in his sense of realism, his ability to interpret the international picture without illusions. He was always clear that it was far easier to change the contents of the Labour wine bottle than the label. The criterion for Party policy, he wrote in May 1943, must be to relate post-war aims to post-war reality. Not only were there the twin dangers of being either too abstract or too precise, there was also the pitfall of being too unchanging. Much of what had previously been said had been rendered obsolete by the war's developments, and he did not exclude his own opinions from this judgement. In September he was to be given the official assignment of preparing a new Party statement on foreign policy. Meanwhile, in May, he composed a personal paper, 'Post-War Aims of the Labour Party',[18] which was circulated among other Labour leaders and certain French Socialists.

Dalton's paper was nothing if not ironic in view of the fact that he had set himself to consider post-war Europe in the light of developments since 1939 and not in terms of pre-war ideas. Essentially his 'reappraisal' represented a reversion to the most extreme anti-Munich position of 1938. The great post-war need now, he believed, was for Anglo-American-Russian co-operation, but his greatest doubts still concerned future United States policy, especially in Europe, and by the end of 1943 these doubts had increased. He continued to maintain that the major post-war European problem would be that of Germany, not of who controlled Germany. What, above all, was needed was a 'Peace of Security', which meant, firstly, that Germany had to be decisively weakened. If the United States were to break loose, it was imperative that closer co-operation with Russia be obtained and, in March 1944, he still believed this would be possible, though difficult. His grounds for this belief were, as he told H. N. Brailsford, who had long been active in Labour Party foreign policy discussions, that the British would have to let the Russians do *most* of what they wanted in Eastern Europe and in Germany. . . .[19]

It was precisely on the last point that the most influential member of the Labour hierarchy consistently favouring a determined attempt to obtain a close understanding with Soviet Russia fell foul of the Party's Left wing. The latter shared neither Dalton's style of *Realpolitik* nor his view of the German problem and its resolution. Yet the more ideologically-minded section of the Party had relatively few positive suggestions to make on the subject. Instead, from May 1943, the revolutionary concept of the war and its resolution received a new impetus. One reason for this was the announcement in Moscow during that month of the dissolution of the Comintern, which the *New Statesman* hailed as 'an event of world importance'. The paper argued that the British Communist Party's latest application for affiliation to the Labour Party should be accepted.[20] *Tribune*, more realistically, was under no illusion that this would happen at the Party conference, or even that a Left-wing attempt to end the electoral truce would be accepted. In fact, both moves were defeated by approximately the same margins – two and a half votes to one.

After the Party conference the Left became more aggressive. Bevan, protesting against the domination of the Party by the TUC, advocated that Labour should become a 'real Federation' of like-minded groups, including some unions, the divisional Labour parties, the ILP, the new Common Wealth Party, a Radical Liberal group, and the Communist Party.[21] The *New Statesman* assailed the Labour leadership, which had ceased to be in any effective way leaders of Labour, though an exception had to be made of Bevin, who had done more for trade-unionists than a Conservative minister would have done. On the 'main issue of strategy and foreign policy' the Labour ministers were urged to recognize that the Allies were drifting apart. The war could easily become a war for Anglo-American domination of the Old Order on the one side and, on the other, a war in which the Soviet Union played a lone hand against Western capitalism. The result, if this continued, was sufficiently obvious and dangerous, the paper considered, to make any responsible leader of Labour ask himself how long it would be possible to be associated with a government the effect of whose long-term policy must be to make the British hesitant leaders of reaction instead of the liberators they proclaimed themselves to be....[22] In short, Dalton, the anti-German, would have accepted Russia's swallowing of Eastern Europe, *faute de mieux*; the Left, carried away by ideological hope, ardently wanted Russian co-operation in Europe in order to ensure the Left's pro-German programme!

Laski, working himself into a nervous breakdown, complained in July that what Labour had failed to learn was that what maintained the authority of the Right was division on the Left,[23] which would appear to be a clear case of the pot calling the kettle black. By August Laski was again in trouble with the NEC. He had published a further attack on Attlee and the leaders of the TUC in an American newspaper, and this had been reported by a British paper. A motion was passed, by 15 votes to 2, empowering the executive to take such steps as it considered necessary 'to dissociate itself from the statements made in the article, in view of Mr Laski's status as a member of the NEC'.[24] Before this could be done the committee learnt that Laski had been taken ill.

There were other reasons for the Left's ideological resurgence from the middle of 1943. The way in which the British and American governments appeared to handle the Italian surrender after the downfall of Mussolini created widespread resentment in the Labour Party. In addition, there was the question of France, and the relationship between de Gaulle and the Allies.[25] To the Left these issues, at the very least, suggested that there was no plan for Europe and, at the worst, that the British and Americans were bent on forestalling revolutionary social and political change in Western Europe. Indeed, even the rump of the parliamentary Labour Party, via Greenwood, asked for a debate on the political aspects of the war situation in July. Replying for the war cabinet, Eden stated that it had been 'unanimously and very definitely' decided that there should be no debate at that stage. This proved to be a tactical error, as Bevan seized the opportunity presented by the open-ended debate on the Consolidated Fund Bill, a few days later, to assail the government. He cited the Darlan episode as an example of why Parliament could not be content with taking the government's word; he hinted, darkly, that there were people who always confused a readiness to destroy the German military army with the fight against Fascism; and finally, he attacked the apparent Allied support for the King of Italy and Marshal Badoglio, begging MPs to realize that what was being done in Italy had important implications for the rest of Europe.[26] But Bevan, and Parliament, had to wait until after the summer recess for Churchill's reply.

During the summer the Left re-stated its thesis, or rather theses, because there were varying approaches, as Bevan himself knew: '. . . the rest of the Labour forces [*ie*, other than the leadership] are divided' he wrote in June, 'whereas at the end of the last war they were united within the Labour Party and the trade unions.'[27] Two basic themes may be distinguished, the one primarily associated with Bevan and his mouthpiece, *Tribune*, the other with Laski and the *New*

Statesman. The basic difference between them lay in their attitude towards Russia; the former, while not unappreciative of the Soviet war effort, always retained an extremely cautious and even detached outlook; whereas the latter tended, with variations, to a positive and optimistic estimate of the possibility, fundamental importance and necessity of good Anglo-Soviet post-war relations. *Tribune* could agree, however, with the *New Statesman*'s criticism of the Coalition government; 'The British,' *Tribune* had declared in May, 'had no foreign policy, only Mr Churchill's intuition.' Yet the paper was alarmed in July by President Roosevelt's loss of control of Congress, compared to which 'the Soviet-Polish conflict was trivial'. It now had to be considered whether the British government should make it clear that, whereas it was prepared to adjust its policies in order to harmonize with those of Roosevelt, it was not prepared to give up its independent conduct of foreign affairs, or to jeopardize its good relations with the European countries, and with the Soviet Union in particular, 'in order to pacify the backwoodsmen of Alabama . . .'. This abandonment of an independent voice could nowhere be better detected than in Britain's handing over her own relations with France to the American State Department and the American army. For *Tribune* the very touchstone of Britain's future good relations with the Continent was France.[28] This emphasis on British independence became later, after further disillusionment with Russia as well as with the United States, *Tribune*'s main contribution to the Labour debate.

When it came, in September 1943, Churchill's parliamentary statement on Italy and the war situation in general, did little to control the groundswell of unease in the Party. The Prime Minister argued that the case of Germany was very different from that of Italy, and he made it clear where his own animosity lay. 'Nazi tyranny and Prussian militarism [were] the two main elements in German life and both must be absolutely destroyed,' he declared. Churchill regarded the conflict about distinguishing between good and bad Germans as academic and sterile. But what was the political motive for the arrangements being made in Italy? Though pressed by such Labour MPs as David Grenfell and Seymour Cocks to say clearly and specifically that the war against Italy had been a war of liberation and whether he intended to allow the Italian emigrés to return, the Prime Minister remained evasive. He also admitted his difficulties with various segments of the French National Committee, but insisted that a strong France and a strong French army was one of the most enduring of British interests. . . .[29]

Perhaps the most significant example of the differing approaches of the two leading Left-wing papers is to be seen in their reactions to the Moscow Conference of Foreign Ministers in 1943. The *New Statesman*'s response was almost euphoric; the partnership had now been converted into a working alliance.[30] This opinion, particularly after the extremely optimistic picture of Allied co-operation painted by Eden in the Commons after his return from Moscow, was widespread. Greenwood (on behalf of the rump PLP) stated that 'no more significant event had taken place in the war . . .'.[31] *Tribune*'s reaction was a good deal more qualified and reserved. It was concerned, in the first place, about Britain's probable post-war economic and strategic weakness which, unless the 'Labour view on foreign policy' prevailed, would mean that Britain alone would not be able to hold a balance between the United States and the USSR. The interests of a free and democratic society in Western Europe, *Tribune* believed, called for the closest co-operation between Britain, France, the Low Countries, Scandinavia and, if possible, a democratic Spain, Italy and Germany. Together they could stand as a friend and aide to the Soviet Union while she built up what the war had destroyed. This was the foreign policy which *Tribune* urged on Labour in October 1943.[32] Consequently, of the Moscow decisions, it was the agreement on the occupation of Italy which received the paper's warmest approval, but even this was marred, in *Tribune*'s eyes, by the lack of any provision for subsequent policy. Soon after, *Tribune* became increasingly sceptical that the Moscow conference had achieved anything significant. Nor did the *New Statesman*'s initial enthusiasm last much longer. The paper conceded that the Soviet Union had an interest in German reparations, but argued that the guiding principle here should be Churchill's – that Germany should be thoroughly disarmed but not impoverished.[33]

So, in the end, it came back to the question of Germany. This was the rock on which the Labour Left-wing hypotheses were fixed and on which they foundered. The 'German question' was a matter of principle on which the Left-wingers would not compromise – neither with fellow Party members, nor with Russia, nor with anyone who appeared to subscribe, directly or indirectly, to the 'guilty nation' theory. Had they been willing to yield on this point, they might have found much firmer support within the Party for a foreign policy perhaps not far removed from that which *Tribune*, the most 'ideologically' consistent paper, enunciated in October 1943. If so, this could conceivably have altered the entire Party and, hence, Coalition situation. As it was, 1943 ended on a note of high irony; 'Critic' of the *New Statesman* expressing much distress at Churchill's illness. 'Many people who are by no means Churchill fans,' he wrote, 'felt their hearts sink last week when they faced the possibility that the country would have to look for a new leader.'[34]

CHAPTER X

The Labour Party and the Post-War International Settlement

So convinced was Dalton of the importance of a decisive reckoning with Germany in the immediate post-war period that, for his part, he was prepared to continue the Coalition, if necessary, in order to achieve it. He believed, in any case, that Churchill and the Conservatives would win an election fought on party lines and found, in 1944, that Attlee considered it would be best if there was no election for six months after the German surrender.[1] Between them, these two men set themselves the task of influencing British policy – Attlee in the realm of government, Dalton primarily in the Labour Party sphere.

The first paragraph of Dalton's original draft of Labour's 'International Post-War Settlement' document dealt with 'Axis Crimes'. He laid great stress on German, as opposed to Nazi, responsibility for these, and pointedly distinguished between German resistance to Fascism and that encountered elsewhere.[2] German national behaviour, he told the International sub-committee of the NEC in January 1944, had provoked five wars since 1864.[3] But this approach proved to be a mistake. Though the committee accepted his proposal that an account of how the German armed forces had behaved in the enslaved countries of Europe should be published separately, and recommended it to the full NEC the following week, much of Dalton's original first paragraph of the 'International Post-War Settlement' never reached the latter body. Moreover, the NEC had something else on its mind: the declaration issued on January 26, 1944 was not about war crimes, but expressed grave concern about the differences that had arisen between the Soviet Union and Poland. The declaration stated that 'a free and independent Poland having its rightful place in any future association of free and peace-loving nations, [was] a vital necessity for post-war Europe'.[4]

This concern was not confined to the Party leadership. If anything, the Left wing of the Party was even more disturbed by the Soviet-Polish dispute – with its direct bearing on the problem of Germany and the wider question of Europe's future. 'If . . . Russia means to force a "friendly" Government on Poland,' *Tribune* warned, 'then she acts no better than any Imperialist Government. . . .' The paper approved of the Curzon line, but condemned the idea of 'compensating' Poland with German territory. This would 'open the floodgates of Partition and Annexation' and would threaten Europe with instability and conflict for another generation.[5] The *New Statesman* agreed, though somewhat more reluctantly. At first, this paper's strictures were largely reserved for the Poles and the idea of the mass transfer of settled populations. The editorial writers were also unhappy now about the systematic destruction of German towns by bombing which, in their opinion, far from producing a Communist revolution would create demoralization and anarchy. By the end of January, however, the *New Statesman* felt obliged to criticize Stalin for his rumoured intention to deal only with a Polish government set up by himself. This rough diplomacy was understandable but dangerous. Power was decisive in the jungle of world politics, but it was not the only influence there.[6]

'Frontiers, migrations, symmetrical maps – why should such things interest us?' H. N. Brailsford plaintively asked, in an article in the same issue. What was needed was the integration of Europe. The wrongs done to the Poles had to be righted, but not by reviving feudal claims of medieval kings. The amends that Germany should make to the Poles should be in the form of machines, electrical equipment and fertilizers, not territory. And, inevitably, this brought Brailsford full circle to the 'other danger' – arising from proposals of which the uncompensated annexation of East Prussia was, for him, a typical instance. True, the corrupted German master race had done immeasurable wrongs to everyone, especially the Slavs. But 'the task', according to Brailsford, was

. . . to plan without passion or hate the European society of tomorrow, knowing full well that it [would] crash unless . . . the Germans [could be included] in it as co-operating members. One day, the Labour Party would have to meet again its former comrades, the Socialist workers of Königsberg. What would it answer them when, as homeless migrants, they quoted the Atlantic Charter?

The *Socialist Commentary* was equally disturbed by the implications of Allied policy towards Germany; dismemberment and destruction of German industry threatened Europe as a whole, it declared.[7] Dalton was thus fated to encounter obstacles with his statement even though, by the middle of January 1944, he had decided to add, 'particularly at the beginning and end, waffling paragraphs to make some feel happy'.[8]

The Left-wing's cup of disillusionment, ironically, was filled to overflowing the following month by Churchill's confirmation of the decision to give East Prussia to Poland and, indeed, his announced support for Russia in general in the Soviet dispute with Poland. If Poland was to get East Prussia, Silesia and Pomerania, declared *Tribune*, 'the devil's broth is started to brew once more even before the old lot has ceased to sizzle'.[9] Both *Tribune* and, from a rather different angle, Stokes,[10] alleged that the connivance of Labour's leadership in all this violated the assumptions and policy on which the Party had entered the Coalition in 1940. The sudden Russian recognition of the Italian government 'of King Victor and Marshal Badoglio' added to the Left-wing's disillusionment with Russia. *Tribune* stated that the Russians had now lined up with Wall Street. They spoke about reparations, territorial claims, national revenge, power politics – 'the old and jarring language of a very old world and of a very old diplomacy'. The paper concluded that 'Labour in Europe and in this country must guard the full independence of its policy'. To win their battles they must look to their own forces and principles. They, at any rate, must not bow to expediency.[11]

Bevan followed this with a detailed analysis and attempt to define, or re-define, 'Labour's European Policy'. Churchill and the Tories had extinguished all signs of a progressive foreign policy, but had not replaced this with one of their own. In this vacuum, the initiative had passed to America and Russia. United States foreign policy was simply British nineteenth-century foreign policy in a modern medium. It obeyed, whether under a Republican or Democratic administration, the outward thrust of American capitalism, and would tend to become imperialistic to the extent that the American people were prepared to lend their bodies to it. Russian policy on the other hand, Bevan believed, was no guide for socialists. The latter ought not to be surprised if Russia still feared a revival of capitalist aggression more than she was reassured by the prospect of the emergence of socialist nations in Europe. Nevertheless, Bevan thought that a socialist integration of

Europe would eventually be recognized by Russia as being in her b~st interests. He therefore urged, more positively than before, 'as a first stage – an organic confederation of the Western European nations, like France, Holland, Belgium, Italy, Spain, the Scandinavian nations along with a sane Germany and Austria and a progressive Britain . . .'. This was the only formula that he could see as likely to assist in laying the foundation for peace and prosperity in Europe. What Eden could not do was to insist that Great Britain was a great power in any sense that included Russia and the United States.[12]

Dalton, meanwhile, had been struggling with his draft Party statement on international policy. By March 14, 1944, he was able to record that it had finally passed through the International sub-committee, but when his revised draft was reviewed by the NEC, in April, he received something of a surprise. It was a 'most remarkable' meeting he noted.[13] Most of 'the pro-Germans' were there, including Noel-Baker, Harold Clay* and Laski. These three, Dalton felt, had already contributed enough in the sub-committee's discussions and 'had never made any direct challenge there to my lay-out'. At the NEC meeting Dalton encountered what he felt was 'obviously pre-arranged . . . sabotage'. Laski, Dalton supposed, had 'No doubt . . . been confabulating with the *New Statesman* crowd, and especially H.N.B. [Brailsford] and K. Martin, and they have told him that my draft is quite frightful'. Noel-Baker said it was 'The wrong sort of draft' and Clay that the beginning was wrong and that it would never get through the annual conference. James Griffiths, whom Dalton considered as 'very wet', was 'horrified' because the Atlantic Charter had not been mentioned, shocked at the paragraph on reparations, and thought that the Labour Party would soon be protesting against the use of forced labour anywhere in Europe: Griffiths moved that the whole draft be referred back. John Parker, a Labour MP who, according to Dalton, had 'taken no effective part in making any alternative proposals' (on the sub-committee), also voted for the reference back. But although Dalton was handicapped by the absence of several of his 'most stalwart supporters' Griffiths's motion was lost by 9 votes to 7. In the light of the further, lengthy discussion of the draft which followed such a close vote it was agreed that members who desired to send in suggestions for amendments should communicate directly with Dalton, that he

* Clay was a leading official of the Transport and General Workers Union and a member of the NEC from 1941–48.

should revise the document and present the revised version to the International sub-committee, and that the sub-committee be empowered to give it final approval.[14]

Considering the, at least, potential importance of the statement this was a remarkably casual way for the Party's executive committee to conduct its business; no doubt the time factor had much to do with it. The decision played into Dalton's hands as he claimed he intended it should. He had himself offered to revise the draft and had sought deliberately 'to implicate Phil [Noel-Baker] and H.J.L. [Laski] by specifically inviting them to redraft certain of the paragraphs to which [he attached] the least importance'. The minority, he believed, were 'rather a cowardly lot', and he was not going to hunt them into the open prematurely. But, his exceptionally long *Diary* entry continued, there might yet be 'a showdown before we are through' – unless the further delay meant that it would not be possible to allow conferences all over the country to discuss the document. Now there would be little time for this, and Dalton's only other worry was that some of the big unions might say that they had not had enough time to consider it. Dalton's further revised version was unanimously cleared for publication on April 18.[15] It had been a long struggle of successive revisions, compromises, and conciliations, he noted, 'but it is not such a bad document'. The 'hard-line' faction had made no mistake about the final meeting and, as Laski and Noel-Baker had contributed 'substantial new sections', Dalton had insisted that the vote be unanimous.[16]

The document – officially a *Report by the NEC of the Labour Party to be presented to the Annual Conference* was published later in April. In summary, the proposals appertaining to Germany were as follows:

(1) Total disarmament, without limit of date.
(2) Occupation for a considerable period.
(3) Destruction of the power of the Junkers, military caste and heavy industrialists.
(4) Some form of international economic controls.
(5) Decisive reduction in 'war potential'.
(6) Swift punishment of war criminals.
(7) A controlled and organized system of reparations and restitution. These were to include reparation in kind, in labour (though not for Britain), and payment of occupation costs. All was to be completed within six years.

(8) The question of frontiers was left open, but all Germans were to go back to the 'post-war' German frontiers.

(9) During the transition period, Germany was not to expect a higher standard of living than her victims, but would share in the eventual upward movement.

That Dalton had largely had his way is clear from the nature of the proposals, the notable absence of any reference to the encouragement of socialist or even trade-union movements in Germany and, above all perhaps, from the section headed 'The Question of German Responsibility'. This section declared flatly that the 'large number of decent, kindly Germans' were 'singularly ineffective in restraining the bad Germans'. Many millions of the latter had been involved in 'The Terror in the Occupied Countries', while most of Hitler's opponents were either dead or had been converted to the Nazi creed. Moreover, a systematic effort had been made since 1933 'to corrupt and brutalize all German youth'. The implication was obvious. Germans were not to be trusted. Therefore, the possibility of future German aggression had to be prevented by 'all necessary measures'. Security was Labour's principal aim in the document as a whole, though the security envisaged was not only against war but also 'against defeat, if war should come, against unemployment, poverty and all other forms of economic distress, and against Fascism and all other forms of political slavery'.

These were large questions, and the tone of the statement became a good deal vaguer on most matters other than that of the German question. It referred to the need, even the necessity, for continued Anglo-American-Russian co-operation; the desirability of a world organization; and the importance of the British Commonwealth and of future international economic organization. There were a few remarks about socialism, together with a categoric assertion that 'pacifism is an unworkable basis of policy'. But, with the sole exceptions of German and Palestinian policy, Labour's 'International Post-War Settlement' added little that was new, contained little that was specific and gave, in effect, *carte blanche* to the Leadership in the field of international affairs. 'The Post-War Settlement must grow out of the immediate Post-War Situation', it declared, in resoundingly Daltonian tones. Just as Labour had entered the Coalition for the prosecution of the War itself, so the Party proposed to approach the Peace – in a spirit of profound pragmatism, except in regard to Germany.

As it turned out, those opposed to the executive's statement were given ample opportunity to organize and voice their criticisms. The annual conference, arranged for May, was postponed until December because of the rocket attacks on London and the advent of D-Day. Nor was opposition slow to manifest itself. As a contribution to the politics of the war, *Tribune* found the document 'deplorable'; its effect on the Germans would be to unite them behind their Nazi masters. The paper sought in vain to find any evidence of 'Socialism' in the document, save in the peroration. The Labour leaders had lost their sense of direction; the Report 'used the language of international co-operation, but [was] an obvious cover for Tory power-politics', a game which Britain was incapable of playing any longer, even if it were desirable. It assumed that the future of the world would be decided by the United States, the USSR and Great Britain; one of 'the most astonishing features was the almost complete absence of any reference to the importance of France in the organization of Europe . . .'.[17] The *New Statesman* took particular offence at the Report's attitude to Germany, which was alien to the whole internationalist tradition of the Party, as was the omission of any reference to the resistance movements in occupied Europe.[18]

In July 1944, the Parliamentary Peace Aims group came to life again, publishing a pamphlet entitled Labour and the Post-War Settlement. The group now described itself as being composed 'exclusively [of] Labour Members of the Lords and Commons, all of whom are deeply disturbed at the handling of these vital issues by the National Executive'. The chairman was the pacifist MP Rhys Davies, the vice-chairman W. G. Cove, and the secretary the indefatigable R. R. Stokes. Their paper was issued, they declared, 'to combat the whole spirit which had animated the N.E.C.'s Report' and, at the same time, 'to restore the traditional policy of our Party in international affairs'. What most worried the group was the Report's attitude to Germany. By September Leonard Woolf, another long-time participant in the formulation of Labour foreign policy, had added his criticism of the Report. He was not so concerned with the executive's aims as the means by which they were to be achieved; these, he believed, should be different from those employed by all other political groups and parties in the Allied nations,[19] though he did not elaborate. *Socialist Commentary* also complained about German policy in October.

The same month, at a Labour Party Policy committee meeting to discuss conference procedure, another attempt was made by Noel-Baker, Laski and Clay to, in Dalton's words, 'dodge our Post-War Settlement document'. The suggestion was made that the Report be split into three sections, the first two dealing with International Policy and International Economic Organization, the third on the 'rest', including the treatment of Germany. This was a transparent effort to isolate the German section from the other items. Dalton countered this suggestion by saying that though the Report might be split into three parts, it would be 'impossible to avoid a straight vote on the declaration as a whole'. It was in vain that Laski attempted to argue that much had happened since the Report had been drafted.[20] The matter was taken to a joint meeting of the Policy and International sub-committees in November but this body finally turned down the suggestion, with the approval of the NEC.[21] 'So we have worn them all down in the end,' Dalton triumphantly commented.[22]

One of the events that had happened, and which Dalton had mentioned in refutation of Laski's argument was the TUC's annual conference.* Although the Presidential address had been considerably more moderate and conciliatory on the question of Germany, the discussion – and the voting – on a summarized report of the Anglo-Soviet Trade Union committee had revealed that the President's attitude was at almost direct variance with that of most delegates.[23] As well, a 'hard-line' attitude towards Germany had been largely confirmed in the Commons, by official spokesmen for the rump Labour opposition. Pethick-Lawrence, in May, stated that he found himself 'in very full agreement' with the Party's statement. It was not necessary to subscribe to the exaggerated view that Germany had been the aggressor all down the Christian era

> . . . to realise the grave crime, the most hideous probably in all history, that has been committed by the German rulers at the present time, for which the instigators must be punished . . . They will have to be punished for their crimes, and the German people as a whole will have to suffer the consequences of steps taken in their name. The innocent as well as the guilty will suffer.[24]

Bevan's position is of special interest as in various ways he succeeded in arousing the antagonism of the entire Labour hierarchy, the British Communist Party and the government. He had been stung, no doubt,

* At Blackpool, October 16–20, 1944.

by Churchill's pronouncement, first made in May,[25] and repeated in August,[26] that the war had become less and less ideological in character. The Parliamentary Labour Party narrowly defeated an attempt to expel Bevan from its ranks early in May[27] and thereafter a joint meeting of the NEC and Administrative committee of the PLP had denounced him for deliberately flouting decisions of the PLP and causing disunity in its ranks.[28] The *Daily Worker* attacked him in July for his opposition to the unconditional surrender policy, and a further joint meeting of the Labour hierarchy, this time including the general council of the TUC, almost expelled him from the Party.[29]

None of this prevented Bevan from bringing his views from the pages of the *Tribune* to the floor of the Commons. In the course of a slashing attack on Churchill, Bevan sarcastically stated that it appeared that there was going to be a general consensus on what they were going to do with the Germans; there would be 'no landlords, no industrial monopolists, no military machine, no Nazis, no reparations and no unemployment . . .'. That was what was needed in Great Britain too! Instead, they were going to 'build up a vast war machine to surround defeated Germany with a sea of tranquillity'. It seemed to him that to be defeated in modern war was better than to win. More seriously, he argued that the maintenance of Britain's own status, and the preservation of whatever contribution it might be able to make to the world, would depend upon the extent to which they could organize around them all the other small nations – so as to try to reduce the importance of armies, navies and air forces. In order to save lives in Europe they had to state some of their terms. But to do that it would be necessary

> . . . to have a man at that [Dispatch] Box who is big enough to lift the eyes of humanity to a far more attractive vision . . . The right hon. Gentleman [Churchill] talked about a campaign here and a campaign there; let the historical chronicler do that. He talked like a second-rate journalist about the difference between ideas and ideology . . .[30]

Yet this speech contained more bark than bite, though the bark appealed hugely to the rank and file. In December, Bevan was elected – by the constituency section of the Party – to the NEC itself.* But by

---

* Bevan came fourth in the ballot, which was again headed by Laski. Bevan took his seat on the NEC on December 13, 1944.

that time he had moderated considerably his remarks on foreign affairs,[31] except on the Greek situation and, here, a large section of the Party outside the government tended to agree with him.

The debate at the annual conference could add little but rhetoric to the moral dilemma that had plagued the Party for so long. Attlee himself moved the resolution welcoming the International Post-War Settlement. And though he did so in the most unprovocative of ways (in the circumstances, that is) he felt obliged to state that the German people as a whole could not be absolved from responsibility, and that restitution and reparations were justifiable demands. Moreover, a great moral and mental revolution, he declared, would be required before the Germans could be trusted again. His speech was mainly notable for his addition of a 're-invigorated France' to the Big Three Powers on whom the future world organization should be based. This offended no one in the Party, and mitigated the somewhat surprising silence on the subject in the NEC's Report. It also denoted something of a change in Attlee's earlier reluctance to commit himself quite so definitely, and no doubt reflected Attlee's cabinet experience (which will be discussed in the following chapter).

An attempt was made at the conference to soften the Party line in regard to Germany but this was unsuccessful and the Report was adopted by an overwhelming majority.[32] 'Thus peacefully ends, for the moment at least, a long controversy' Dalton confided to his *Diary*. 'I have got my way on all essentials.'[33] Clearly he had, but equally clearly, on the German issue his way was the direction in which the Party as a whole wanted to be pointed. If Dalton manipulated opinion, that he succeeded so well was due at least as much to the fact that the Party shared his views in this respect, as to his own considerable efforts.

It remains to be emphasized that the 1944 conference was most exercised in the field of foreign affairs by the then current controversy over Greece – though this itself might be seen as a measure of the general agreement over German policy. In a Commons debate on Greece, just before the conference, the government had only managed to secure a 279–30 vote, with a large number of Labour MPs being among the abstainers. The difficult task of defending the government's policy at the conference fell to Bevin. It was, Dalton unwittingly noted, 'a most powerful and persuasive speech', and demonstrated that 'Bevin had very great power in this Conference'.[34] It was this power (which, of course, was not merely or mostly oratorical) which was to sustain

Bevin in the post-war years when he was Foreign Secretary, and was almost certainly one of the two major factors influencing Attlee in his selection of Bevin, rather than Dalton, for the post.*

Labour's pronounced capacity for sudden or sustained moral excitement probably served to obscure the development of a deeper and more comprehensive discussion of the European problem during the war. Just as the immediate issue of Greece, in December 1944, tended to divert the attention of the Party from the German question, so too had the previous preoccupation – almost an obsession – with the latter circumscribed the debate on the wider problem of Europe's future. The end result was that the leadership obtained sweeping powers of interpretation of Party foreign policy, while yielding little on the moral plane. In particular, the policy enunciated by Bevan and *Tribune*, though it exaggerated the extent to which a more independent policy might have been pursued by Britain within the Grand Alliance, received nothing like the attention it might be supposed to have merited. The leadership had not been much concerned even to exploit the stresses and strains on the Left. But it should also be noted that during 1944 the most important of the Labour leaders were, in any case, more preoccupied with the formulation of government rather than Party policy.

* The other was Attlee's decision to separate, as much as possible, Bevin and Morrison, who were mutually antagonistic.

CHAPTER XI

Attlee over Germany

CLEMENT ATTLEE'S unprepossessing appearance and manner were nothing if not deceptive. Taciturn and reserved, he had become leader of his querulous, loquacious and turbulent Party virtually by accident during a period when all authority within the Party was more or less suspect. From a position well to the left of centre he had, over the years, come to occupy one in the middle of Labour's political spectrum. Though almost incapable of arousing any emotional enthusiasm, he enjoyed the confidence and loyalty of the majority of the PLP. Indeed, in a Party not lacking prima donnas, his colourless, even drab personality had a curious appeal; the fact that he retained his leadership for so long may have been due, to some extent, to his very diffidence.

By 1944, however, he had begun to make his mark, even if only among a few. In contrast to Churchill, he was efficient and business-like in cabinet and in 1945 protested to the Prime Minister about the latter's shortcomings in this respect.[1] Overworked and exhausted civil servants and generals were increasingly appreciative of these qualities. It was discovered that he was a good committee man and an excellent chairman.[2] He could be relied upon to take a 'balanced' view; he knew how to get a consensus; he was decisive. Only later was it remarked that he was an extremely adroit, calculating politician, that he did not suffer fools gladly, that he had a streak of ruthlessness,[3] and that he had rather strong views on certain subjects. One of the latter was Germany; it was no fault of his that the Armistice and Post-War committee (and the government) were still undecided at the end of the year about long-term policy on this subject.

The new terms of reference and revised composition of the Armistice Terms and Civil Administration committee of the war cabinet which Attlee had devised and secured in November 1943, did not suffice for long. The committee met only five times in the early part of 1944.

before being superseded by a new body. During these meetings not much was added to what had been decided about Germany, supposedly for the short term, the previous December. The draft German armistice was approved, and it was agreed that the document should be submitted as a basis for discussion to the European Advisory Commission, Moscow, Washington, the chiefs of staff and the governments of the Dominions. In effect, the draft simply put everything – and everybody – in Germany, at the disposal of the Allies. Even so, it hardly went far enough for Attlee. He was concerned at the suggestion, for instance, that the German police should be allowed to function, in order to avoid a general paralysis of life in Germany. Instead, he intimated it would be better if police duties were taken out of German hands altogether.[4] Later, the issue of whether to make all German Forces p.o.w.s at the end of the war arose; this stemmed from a proposal by the Russians who were not signatories to the Geneva Convention. A committee of officials had been unable to agree about this because, if made p.o.w.s, the Germans would promptly claim the protection of the Convention, which the British neither wanted nor could afford. They knew they would be unable to feed all the Germans. Attlee's curt comment was that public opinion would not be very aggrieved at whatever might happen to the Germans; they had enslaved millions of the inhabitants of Europe, and thus would only be getting just retribution. The committee decided to ask the Russians to avoid using the term 'p.o.w.s'.[5] Attlee further emphasized his views concerning the post-war representation of the Dominions on Allied bodies; specifically, he suggested that the Canadians be represented at the highest level (*ie*, the Allied High Commission) in Germany during the occupation period or, if this was not possible, then certainly at staff level.

In April 1944, this committee was given a new name, the Armistice and Post-War committee, and much wider terms of reference. Attlee remained chairman, and Bevin was among seven ministers who were always to be invited to attend.[6] The APW committee was intended to be a key decision-making body, not only in regard to German policy in the short and long terms, but also in regard to the entire post-war European settlement. To it reported the British representative on the EAC, William Strang, and, in addition, the committee served as the clearing house for the various specialized and inter-departmental committees of officials, the Foreign Office and the chiefs of staff. By the end of the year the APW committee had received and considered no fewer than 127 memoranda, reports and papers, and had met some twenty-three times. No better committee chairmanship for a future Prime Minister could have been devised!

One of the earliest decisions made by the APW committee was to instruct Strang to press for some Armistice provision concerning the disbandment of the German armed forces and also for some provision for 'territorial changes', if these were thought necessary. The latter was tantamount to expanding the terms of reference of the EAC, and Strang soon reported that neither the USSR nor the United States was willing to agree. Hence the committee decided not to press the matter. Instead, in regard to the President's proposal that the British and American zones be switched, there was 'complete agreement' that the political arguments for the British occupying the north-west of Germany were just as strong as the military reasons. British vital interests were at stake; it was essential that the north-west European Powers be held tightly to Britain. The committee were fully aware that the demand for north-west Germany also involved a decision about Europe. Equally, it was maintained that there could be no giving way to the Russians on the question of the participation by the smaller powers in the occupation of Germany. Here, the emphasis was put upon the necessity for the conservation of British manpower; to this end, Allied contingents would be necessary.[7]

But while Attlee agreed with, and endorsed, these decisions *about* Germany, he became increasingly irritated by certain proposals reaching his committee on what should be done inside 'Germany' after the war. In June he expressed these feelings by directing a memorandum over the heads of his committee to the full war cabinet. This dealt with 'The Treatment of Major War Criminals';[8] in Attlee's opinion a list prepared by Eden should be expanded. It was a mistake to confine the list exclusively to Nazi Party members; he suggested that those members of the German armed forces who had prepared and planned major criminal acts, such as the bombing of Rotterdam, should be included. And he re-iterated that the Junker class had to be dispossessed of their estates. By July, Attlee's irritation reached a climax and the matter came to a head in the APW committee. His differences with Eden had become evident before the meeting. On July 11, Attlee circulated a paper to the members of the committee entitled 'Policy Towards Germany'.[9] One of the papers to be considered at the next meeting, he pointed out, was a Report by an inter-departmental committee, under Foreign Office chairmanship, on the transfer of German populations. This set out the problems which would arise if the German inhabitants of Czechoslovakia and of a Poland extended westward to the Oder river, were expelled and transferred to the rump Germany. The maximum figure involved was about 10 million people. The general tenor of the Report was that transfers on that scale would impose such hardships on Germany – the lack of homes, work and food for such an influx – as to create insuperable economic difficulties which might well lead to a complete German collapse.

Attlee conceded that the issues raised in the Report were of very great importance. They included such questions as the dismemberment of Germany, the handling of the Sudetenland, the future of Poland and so on. But before the merits of the Report were examined, Attlee thought that there was a fundamental point which had to be brought out into the open and dealt with. It concerned not only this Report but others and had already come into indirect prominence in previous documents, such as those on the disbandment of Nazi organizations and the paper on the German police. Attlee then stated his point as follows:

It is universally agreed that the object of occupying Germany is to ensure that by no possible means shall Germany re-emerge in the foreseeable future as a menace to peace and security. The surrender terms to Germany have been drawn up in such a way as to give the Allies complete power in Germany, so that they will be able to achieve this object. We are now engaged in working out policy and in framing directives, so that we can make up our minds how best to proceed in Germany when we have occupied that country, and to ensure that our military commanders act accordingly. The point at issue is which should be the dominant note in that policy and those directives. Should it be: (*a*) that, subject to the disarmament and demilitarization of Germany, the restoration of normal, orderly and organized life in Germany should be brought about as quickly as possible and that Germany should be provided with food and facilities for economic, commercial and industrial revival; or should it be: (*b*) that at all costs Nazi influence and the German warlike cult must be utterly rooted out, even if the result at first is that Germany will feel the full impact of military defeat, including loss of territory influx of transferred populations, political and economic turmoil and so on?*

Attlee made it plain that he favoured the second course, despite the fact that it seemed to him 'that the papers now coming up before the committee are all based on the first hypothesis'. He took it for granted that a situation of chaos and economic disorganization inside Germany would have to be avoided in so far as it was detrimental to British interests elsewhere. Nor could ordinary considerations of humanity be left entirely out of account. On the other hand, the proper criterion to be applied in these matters for him was 'not how hardly will a particular course of action bear upon Germany, but how far can we go in the direction of achieving our desiderata in Germany without serious embarrassment or injury to ourselves?' It was relevant that probably ninety per cent of the area and population affected by transfers would fall within the Russian zones, and they could be certain that the Russians would not be disposed to any policy of appeasement or undue consideration for German feelings or interests. The approach embodied in the Report seemed to him to be open to objection on these grounds.

Attlee referred to what, in his opinion, had happened after the last war. Stability had been quickly restored – and the field had been prepared for the growth of militaristic ideas, at first clandestinely, then blatantly in the open. This time, there would be total occupation, but the natural British and American tendency was to relapse into a peaceful neutrality which could easily lead to the same result as the last time. He concluded, it was vital that 'we should be quite uncompromising in the early stages, when the realisation of German enormities [would be] still vivid, in our measures for eradicating the whole German military machine and the whole Nazi system, root and branch'. Such a policy might carry certain risks of precipitating an internal crisis; the people might be subjected to great hardship.

But even if one does not take an extreme view of the responsibility of the German people for our trials, one can still argue that everything that brings home to the Germans the completeness and irrevocability of their defeat is worthwhile in the end.

The provisions of the Atlantic Charter were no obstacle to such a

* This quotation is reproduced by permission of the Controller of Her Majesty's Stationery Office.

policy, and the only alternative would be a prolonged occupation for, say, thirty years. It would be a forlorn hope to imagine that either America or Britain would have the necessary toughness in peace-time to carry that through. If they were not careful, the Germans would get away with it once again. What, after all, did they mean by re-establishing a 'normal' Germany? Apart from the Nazis, the two enduring factors in German national life for the past fifty years had been the Prussian military land-owning caste, and the controllers of heavy industry, who looked to war or the apprehension of war to provide them with orders. In Attlee's view, before restoring any self-government to Germany, the former had to be dealt with, and the taking away of East Prussia would be a help. Nor should the heavy industries be allowed to remain in the hands of the present owners. Plans ought to be worked out for the plant and workers to be employed under international control for the rehabilitation of devastated Europe. The economic power which made aggression possible for the military had to be rendered safe.

Eden took the unusual course of responding to this paper before the APW committee met. He hoped that the committee would take his word for it that the Foreign Office had no more tender feelings for such elements as the Junkers and industrialists – whom it regarded as the most dangerous enemies – than had any other section of the British public. The sole reason that certain Nazi organizations, though purged, might be temporarily retained was to avoid chaos. Eden indicated in some detail, that, though he agreed with Attlee about an uncompromising policy in the early stages, he disagreed with Attlee's proposed method.[10]

The resulting APW committee's discussion[11] of these papers served merely to reveal still further the underlying differences of opinion. Bevin now stated that there was much to be said for dealing with the German States and returning to the Germany of Bismarck. He believed that in these States there was a good deal of suppressed ability and skill in existence which could be re-created. If they dealt with the central government of Germany they would be accepting the system set up by the Nazis; to preserve that system would be to prepare the way for another war. Yet it would be found impossible for any other central machine to emerge as an alternative to the Nazi State. Attlee agreed; the difference of opinion was precisely on the question of the central machine which he felt ought to be smashed. Bevin added that the acceptance of a formal surrender by the German government did not bind them to preserve that government. . . . The trend of the discussion so perturbed the chief official present, Strang, that he reminded ministers that if they did not want to work through a central German bureaucracy, it would be necessary to reconstruct the policy hitherto advanced in the EAC. . . . The main idea in their papers was that there would be a tripartite authority to control Germany, which would work through the German civil government, and which would be constructed to fit the organization of that government. . . . The argument in favour of such a form of control was that you could disarm Germany and destroy the Nazi system more easily and effectively. In any case, the occupation of Germany was to be in zones demarcated in such a way as to suit a dismemberment of Germany into three parts. This last remark was so frank that Eden felt obliged to shift his ground. Instructions could be issued to Strang to advocate all possible measures to promote the division of Germany into States. The Secretary of State for War, Sir James Grigg, also suggested that a study should be made of what changes in their plans would be necessary if there was no formal surrender by Germany, and with this and Eden's previous comment there was general agreement. Clearly, the views of the Labour ministers had carried a certain amount of conviction – so much so that Eden noted that his aim of demilitarizing Germany would require further expansion.

Before the APW committee's next meeting, Eden – apparently disturbed by the trend of the previous discussion – had written to Attlee[12] proposing amendments to the 'conclusions' then reached. Explaining these amendments to the committee on July 27,[13] the Foreign Secretary said that two points were of fundamental importance. Firstly, on the question of dismemberment, Eden stressed that no one had yet gone beyond saying 'encourage'. He would like to see it come from within, and doubted that it would be of any use if brought about by force. In regard to the dissolution of the central machinery of the German government, Eden was anxious about the short-term consequences. How, for example, could Three Power control work in the beginning? More study was needed. Attlee and Bevin had no objections to this, and the committee agreed to suspend judgement on the matters raised in Attlee and Eden's memoranda until the various reports on dismemberment were available for consideration. Other members of the committee, however, indicated that they were already decided upon a definite dismemberment.

In August the APW committee addressed itself to the question of economic policy in Germany. Bevin suggested that the extent to which German industry had expanded and developed for purely war purposes before the war should be ascertained and that this should thereafter be reduced to an appropriate peace-time level. Dalton, who was present while this item was discussed, went a good deal further. He argued that it would not be in British interests to promote Germany's recovery in advance of that of the Allies, and expressed his unease at the phrase used recently by the United States government about their anxiety to 're-start German trade after the war'. A list of German industries to be completely eliminated had already been prepared by the officials and he cautioned against any omissions from this list being too lightly made – in view of the difficulty of foreseeing technical developments. The committee sided eventually with Oliver Lyttelton, the Minister of Production, and with Eden. Lyttelton had proposed a 'draconian policy towards selected fields of German production' because if they tried to destroy every aspect of it, they would defeat their own ends. Accordingly the committee directed Eden to have a new list drawn up of industries to be completely eliminated. It was also decided that such measures would not be limited to the period of occupation, which, anyway, would be for a minimum of ten years.[14]

Between the APW committee's meetings at the end of August and one held on September 21, 1944, the Anglo-American Conference at Quebec was held. It was at this conference that both Churchill and Roosevelt initialled the Morgenthau plan – the proposal of the US Secretary to the Treasury that Germany be transformed into a basically agricultural state. Details of the so-called plan were leaked to the British before the Quebec meeting in an attempt, not so extraordinary at the time, to persuade the British to prevail upon the President to reject it.[15] On the very day the conference opened, September 11, the cabinet (in the absence of Churchill and Eden) asked the Foreign Office to send a message to Eden, who in turn was to deliver it to the Prime Minister. The terms of the message were agreed between Attlee, the Chancellor of the Exchequer, the Secretary of State for War, the Minister of Production and the vice-chiefs of staff, though not Bevin. The Morgenthau plan, the message argued,[16] would be wholly against British interests because (1) the task of the occupation forces would thereby be made more difficult, and more forces would be needed; (2) a few profiteers would gain and the true sufferers would be the middle and working classes; (3) the British name would be associated with avoidable and purposeless suffering and not with just retribution; and (4) all hope of getting an adequate contribution out of Germany towards reconstruction of Europe would vanish. A policy which condoned or favoured chaos would not be hard, simply inefficient. The cabinet did not favour a soft policy towards Germany, but the suffering which she must undergo should be the price of useful results for the United Nations, ordered and controlled by the British. The message sent to Churchill noted that Bevin was not prepared to commit himself to these views without more knowledge of the President's proposals and a fuller examination of the arguments against them. Attlee's position can be easily defined. Although he wanted a three-way dismemberment (at least), and a thorough social and political purge of Germany – for which he was willing to take the *risk* of chaos if necessary – he did not countenance the economic smashing of Germany for its own sake.

While Eden was still *en route* to the conference, Churchill informed the war cabinet that though he was first taken aback by Morgenthau's plan he now thought the argument made to him about disarming Germany decisive and that the beneficial consequences to Great Britain would follow naturally.[17] That same day, September 15, he initialled the plan. Attlee drew the attention of the APW committee at its meeting on September 21 to what had happened at Quebec and serious doubts were expressed as to the practicability of the proposals.[18] An officials' report was called for, and when it appeared in December, these doubts were confirmed and amplified. A further attempt by Morgenthau, via Lord Cherwell, the Prime Minister's chief scientific adviser, and Churchill himself, to influence British occupation policy, which had been examined and approved in detail by Attlee's committee was thwarted by both the Foreign Office and the War Office.[19]

Churchill's action at Quebec, against the wishes of the cabinet and Foreign Office, has aroused some speculation. One theory has it that the simple arithmetic of Morgenthau's plan, in Churchill's mind, added up to the promotion of British economic recovery at the expense of Germany,[20] and that this appealed to the President.[21] It is also possible to view Churchill's deference to Roosevelt in this matter in the wider context of the Prime Minister's general desire for the furtherance of post-war Anglo-American co-operation because, at this juncture, the President had not yet spoken of his intention to withdraw American troops from Europe after the war.[22] Churchill, moreover, had two other European objectives at Quebec: to secure American aid for Britain after the war and to persuade Roosevelt that the British zone of occupation should be the north-western region. Churchill achieved the creation of an Anglo-American committee (with Morgenthau as president) to study the former, and got his way completely on the second point. Attlee's and the cabinet's satisfaction at the overall result of the Quebec Conference was in relation to these objectives, and also to the arrangements made for mutual lease-lend during the period between the surrender of Germany and the surrender of Japan – which everyone assumed would occur far later than it did. There is no evidence in British sources to support Cordell Hull's contention that the offer of assistance was in return for British acceptance of the Morgenthau plan. Much more likely is it that the American agreement on the zonal allocations which had been signed at the EAC in London on September 12 would have loomed larger in Churchill's mind. It certainly did in the minds of Attlee's committee.[23] Earlier that month the committee had received a further communication from the chiefs of staff[24] which upheld, in no uncertain terms, the position adopted by the military advisers in the previous July.

The chiefs of staff now indicated in detail their belief that dismemberment of Germany – with the British retaining control of the north-western sector – was not only desirable to prevent any renewal of German aggression, but also necessary as an insurance against the possible hostility of Russia. If Russia should turn hostile it would involve a complete reorientation of military and political policy in Europe, the Middle and Far East, including the support of Germany. As it was unlikely that the USSR would ever permit the rearming of a united Germany which she did not dominate, the only alternative would be the hope of bringing north-western and perhaps southern Germany into a west European orbit. Dismemberment would also reduce the likelihood of the whole of Germany combining with the USSR against Great Britain, which the chiefs of staff feared more than anything else. In the immediate future they favoured as much dismemberment as might be economically feasible and warned that the ruthless use of armed force might be required to secure this. These recommendations met all of Attlee's main points, except that of an internal social and economic purge. Nor were they far removed from the Foreign Office's view of the three occupation zones outlined earlier by Strang. Nevertheless the chiefs of staff now fell foul of Eden. General

Ismay, their secretary and also Churchill's personal representative, informed a meeting of the chiefs on October 6, that the Foreign Secretary was of the opinion that it would pay the British not to dismember Germany, and the chiefs had thereupon approached the Prime Minister. Churchill's response was that he understood that both President Roosevelt and Marshal Stalin were in favour of dismemberment and went even further in the matter than he (Churchill) was prepared to go. He undertook to talk the matter over with Eden.[25]

What had really annoyed the Foreign Office was the blunt military argument that a part of Germany could be used, if necessary, against a combination of East Germany and Russia. This, the Foreign Office retorted, was 'fantastic and dangerous'. Dismemberment would be regarded by British and American opinion as an injustice, the Foreign Office believed, and the Germans would try to evade it. British policy was to preserve the unity and collaboration of the United Nations. To plan with the idea that Germany might serve as part of an anti-Soviet alliance would destroy any hope of maintaining the Anglo-Soviet alliance and would entail a relaxation of disarmament and other measures designed to prevent future German aggression. Even if the Russians wanted dismemberment (the Moscow meeting in October was to reveal that Stalin's opinion was unchanged) and suspected British opposition to it, the British should continue to oppose it. However, it was emphasized that the rejection of dismemberment did not mean leaving Germany in its present centralized state. The dissolution of Prussia could be achieved; German industry could be internationally controlled; and a return to a federal system or even a system of decentralization would diminish the authority of the central government. Subsequent meetings of the APW committee have to be viewed against the background of the dispute between the Foreign Office and the chiefs of staff. After the Churchill-Eden visit to Moscow, in October 1944, the chiefs of staff declared that while they hoped for the maintenance of friendship with Russia and the success of the world security organization, they were obliged to consider every possibility. The Foreign Office insisted that if the Russians thought the British were trying to build a bloc against them, co-operation would be impossible.[26]

The APW committee[27] had no difficulty deciding that it was essential to have a recorded agreement between the Three Powers that there would be common use of the airfields in the Greater Berlin area, but the question of the control machinery in Germany was a different matter. Strang informed the committee that both the United States and the USSR thought that they had to start with the idea that a central German administration would exist for the tripartite authority to work through, at least at the outset. G. H. Hall, the Parliamentary Under-Secretary of State for Foreign Affairs, who was a Labour MP, confirmed that Eden had discussed this with Churchill at Quebec and was of the same opinion. A report by the officials' committee on Armistice Terms and Civil Administration[28] lent strong support to these statements. Nevertheless, Attlee continued to advocate that there must be the intention of decentralizing the German administration even if such a body was used at first, and that plans should be based on the establishing of provincial or local administrations. And Bevin maintained his view that if once they came to rely upon a central German administration they would never be able to break it down later. He thought it would pay them to set up a separate administration in the Ruhr as soon as possible. The population in that area, which included many former trade union members, might well be glad to be separated from Prussia at once.

The committee was obliged to compromise. It was decided that the EAC should still work on the assumption that there would be a central German administrative machine through which the Allied authority could function initially. Nevertheless, the control machinery should be made sufficiently flexible to permit adjustments to meet the requirements of other conditions or other policies. After this, the committee agreed that the length of military control of Germany should be as short as possible. The chief British objectives during this period were identified as the disarmament of Germany; the abolition of the Nazi régime; the preparation of conditions for the creation in Germany of organs based on democratic principles; and the beginning (though not necessarily the completion) of the most urgent tasks of economic disarmament. By late November 1944, Bevin was becoming weary of the problem of Germany. He told the committee that a great deal of study and attention was being devoted to the latter after defeat, and careful plans were being made for her control. He felt considerable anxiety as to whether enough attention was being paid to the problems of the Allied liberated countries. He feared that all the thought being given to German problems would result in her difficulties being solved at the expense of, and before, those of the rest of Europe.[29]

Right up to the Yalta Conference (February 1945), however, it was

the Labour ministers who continued to play the role of chief protagonists in regard to German policy, Attlee, Bevin and Dalton being
joined by A. V. Alexander, the First Lord of the Admiralty. Alexander,
on January 3, 1945, sent a memorandum[30] to the APW committee
urging that the question of German industry as a whole be tackled
before that of specific areas or industries. Germany's industrial future,
Alexander believed, had also to be viewed in the light of British
reconstruction plans. He was very critical of a report by the officials
for giving too much weight to 'subsidiary factors' such as interference
with reparations, shrinkage of German export markets, possible German unemployment and probable defaulting on British investments in
Germany. Security against future war was the first priority. This might
demand sacrifices from German and British sectional interests, in the
latter case capitalists. There ought not to be undue concern for the
standard of living of the German people. Second only to the primary
interest of British military security was the need to reconstruct British
industries. But when the committee met on the following day, it
merely agreed that to pastoralize the Rhineland-Westphalia-Saar area
would not provide a solution to the problem of preventing future
German aggression.[31]

The APW committee's final meeting[32] before the Yalta Conference
found all the Labour ministers present, Attlee, Alexander and Dalton,
adamant that British pre-war claims on Germany should rank behind
those for British reparations. Here they succeeded in obtaining a compromise very much orientated towards their point of view. Dalton
again overstepped the mark in regard to a second topic. As President
of the Board of Trade he spoke in his official capacity on the subject of
British civil requirements from Germany. The British, he hoped, were
not going to put any raw materials into Germany, save perhaps in the
most exceptional cases and for specific purposes. His idea was to get
raw materials such as timber, potash and steel, as well as plant and
machinery, out of Germany. The British aim, he declared, should be to
weaken Germany by extracting equipment from her to build up
Britain's own industrial resources. This brought a reaction from Oliver
Lyttelton, who emphasized that British claims on German industry did
not conflict with the British plan for economic security. Dalton's
proposal would result in a complete crippling of German industry on
the lines of the Morgenthau plan. They should only remove plant from
those industries selected for elimination. At this, Dalton explained that

his intention was that reparations should be exacted in kind rather than in money values. By this method it would be the British who would decide what was taken out of Germany, whereas if a total claim was made the Germans would be able to choose in what form the claims should be met. The committee's conclusion from this contretemps was to set up an inter-departmental committee to prepare lists, and this body was to include someone from the Dominions Office.

Prior to Yalta the net result of all the work of the APW committee was that there was still no agreed, far-reaching British policy for Germany. But the short-term policy originated at the end of 1943 had not only been clarified but had also been remarkably successful in terms of its acceptance by Russia and the United States, who had been joined by the French. Moreover, this 'short-term' policy corresponded very closely to what Attlee and Bevin had advocated as a long-term objective. It accorded well with the formal expression of Party policy which had been enunciated at the end of 1944, and had received the blessing of the military authorities. The subsequent international stalemate, and the resulting breakdown of the proposed tripartite control of Germany, only served to bring the Labour leaders' goal of a truncated or 'dismembered' and a disarmed, socially transformed 'Germany' that much nearer.

CHAPTER XII

From Teheran to Yalta: The Labour Cabinet Ministers and the rest of British European Policy

THE major reason why the British cabinet was unable to work out a long-term policy towards Germany in 1944 was that there was no international agreement about the political future of Europe as a whole. The discussions at Moscow and Teheran in 1943 had been inconclusive, though the possibility, at least, of a more permanent collaboration between the United States and the USSR could not be ruled out. It had been the Marshal and the President, after all, who had personally fixed the date of Overlord. Awareness of this possibility added urgency to the British effort to arrive at a more satisfactory definition of European policy. Yet the leading British politicians did not succeed in this endeavour prior to the Yalta Conference; they could not agree among themselves or by themselves. The fact was that the British cabinet's decisions and policy on Germany and Europe were neither sovereign nor autonomous but strictly dependent on the United States and USSR. In the last analysis there were too many variables in the situation which could only be resolved, if at all, round an international conference table. And although 1944 was a momentous year on the battlefield, it was considerably less so at the conference table.* In both arenas the soldier's voice was to count as much as the politician's, which appeared to be the last thing the British could want. The paucity of Britain's military power, actual and potential – relative to that of the super-powers – cried out for redress at the political level. Significantly, it was Churchill and Eden who did the travelling, both to Moscow and North America, in the course of the year.

In March Attlee and Bevin again demonstrated their complete accord with an aspect of traditional British policy – the preservation of British

---

* Apart from the work of the EAC and, in August, the Dumbarton Oaks Conference, no top-level tripartite meetings at all were held in 1944.

interests in south-eastern Europe. Bevin made a point of attending the Armistice Terms and Civil Administration committee meeting[1] at which a Foreign Office report on this subject was submitted. Three 'Inescapable Commitments' were listed: a free and independent Austria, occupation of the Dodecanese Islands to prevent a Greek-Turkish-Italian conflict, and Greece, where the commitment was to be limited to a military mission. Here, there was also a separate proposal – for a small combatant force to be stationed temporarily in Athens 'to support the interim Greek administration'. In addition, the report listed four 'desirable commitments'; these included the north-east Italian frontier, a free and independent Albania, and Bulgaria, if she came to terms with the Allies before the end of the war. If not, Russia would claim a large share of the occupation. British interests lay 'in preventing the extension of Soviet influence towards the Straits and the Mediterranean', but there could be no British occupation of Bulgaria except in agreement with the Russians. The same applied to the fourth 'desirable commitment', Hungary. Attlee's committee did not merely accept this report; it also suggested that the word 'desirable' be changed to 'probable'. On the question of Austria, however, it was agreed that the Soviet proposal at the EAC for a tripartite occupation be accepted, but only because it might help to bring the United States into the area. These were large commitments.

In July, perhaps because of his knowledge of the probable post-war British manpower situation, Bevin informed the committee that he wanted to see both the United States and the USSR take only a very small part in Austrian affairs. He strongly favoured a customs union between all the smaller states of southern Europe, including Austria, directed southwards towards the Mediterranean, where he hoped Britain would play the major role.[2]

By the summer of 1944, it had become evident that the demands of the traditional imperial role would necessitate severe restrictions on what Britain could do elsewhere. The Armistice and Post-War committee, consequently, was obliged to change its mind about Bulgaria and Hungary, though adhering staunchly to the policy for Greece.[3] Attlee presented his committee with a memorandum entitled 'Manpower One Year After the Defeat of Germany – Decisions Required from H.M.G.'*[4], which, in effect, superimposed his own comments on a similar memorandum emanating from the chiefs of staff. He suggested

* His Majesty's Government.

that the committee might accept the chiefs' view that the only part of Italy which would require military occupation would be the north-eastern frontier zone, where some 23,300 men would probably be needed. Attlee noted that the chiefs had drawn attention to the close interest in Hungary that was shown in certain British circles and that, in the circumstances, the case for a token force there was a strong one. Regarding Bulgaria, however, he made it clear that this would be a Russian area, and that Britain's estimated contribution of 46,000 troops might be substantially reduced. The committee[5] agreed with all Attlee's suggestions, though in the case of Hungary a final decision on the exact manpower figure was postponed. They also agreed with the chiefs of staff's figures for the 'inescapable' commitments – Austria 23,000; north-eastern frontier zone of Italy 23,300; the Dodecanese 1,200; and Greece 10,000. Attlee stressed that everything possible should be done to associate their European allies in the task of occupying ex-enemy countries; the main difficulty was how to overcome the opposition of the Soviet government. The only Dominion forces envisaged for use in Europe, the committee was informed, were Canadian; some 25,000 troops, some minesweepers and corvettes, and eleven squadrons of planes: there would be nothing from Australia or New Zealand, except for a token force of one or two air squadrons. Indeed, the entire strategic imperial reserve that the chiefs of staff were able to allocate would consist of thirty heavy bomber squadrons in Britain and the Middle East, and some 165,500 men in the latter area.

At the committee's next meeting,[6] these agreements were all confirmed, and the chiefs were informed that there was no need for them to be referred to the full war cabinet; they could proceed on the basis of the committee's recommendations. The latter also included an agreement that no troops at all need be provided for Bulgaria.

Russian policy was not seen as an insuperable obstacle. The official British view in 1944 was that, far from threatening British interests, Russia could be expected to pursue a generally co-operative policy in the immediate post-war era. A top-secret Foreign Office assessment[7] expressed the view that from the peace settlement onwards, any possible friction between Britain and Russia would be likely to arise not so much out of ideological disagreements, but chiefly because Britain and Russia might take different views about the post-war treatment of Germany. The only circumstance in which the Soviet government might take the risk of seeking Germany's friendship was if they were to convince themselves that Britain and the United States had reversed their present policy and were building up Germany as a defence against the Soviet Union, and if they felt confident of Russia's recovery of strength and ability to remain the dominant partner. Unless these conditions were fulfilled it seemed very improbable to the Foreign Office that Russia would welcome even a Communist Germany. Ironically, the essence of this report was given to the cabinet by Eden in August 1944,[8] at a time when the idea of a Western European bloc was being actively canvassed and receiving a good deal of official support. But Foreign Office advocacy of some form of regional grouping in Western Europe fell short of the idea of including Germany. The emphasis was placed, instead, on the contribution such a grouping would make to the machinery of a world organization security system though, admittedly, a Western bloc would provide an insurance against the failure of such a system. A Western European grouping, moreover, would enable Britain to play a more effective part in the world organization. The Anglo-Soviet Treaty remained the basis of the whole of British policy for Europe and everything possible had to be done to reinforce it. The Foreign Office contended that the formation of some west European system would do just this.[9]

Both Attlee and Bevin (and, indeed, all the Labour ministers) had expressed solid support throughout the war for a resurgent France, and also for the France represented in the short term by de Gaulle.[10] On the question of a west European bloc, however, Attlee and Bevin diverged somewhat in the middle of 1944. Bevin resolutely backed a world organization. The latter possibility had come before the Armistice and Post-War committee for the first time in April, and Lyttelton had indicated that the chiefs of staff were not prepared to go in wholeheartedly for a world security system. This had provoked an immediate response from Bevin; Lyttelton's suggestion was one that he could not possibly accept. It was essential to make a really great effort to obtain such a system, without which they would merely be heading straight for the next war. However, he was not willing to subscribe to any such system which did not have force behind it. Either they went in whole-heartedly, and made clear to the Dominions and the Americans what was involved, or they must tell people that no scheme of world security was practicable.[11]

The Armistice and Post-War committee's eventual report to the war cabinet[12] recommended a body presumably to Bevin's satisfaction. There should be a world council consisting of some nine to twelve members, of which four had to be the Great Powers. A two-thirds majority should be necessary for the settlement of non-justiciable disputes and the use of force, and in these cases the majority must always include the Big Four, none of whom could abstain. Nor should there be any right of withdrawal from the council, which should be established before the peace settlement. Nothing was said about a European or any other regional council as this was still under discussion. By November, Churchill had pronounced himself in favour of Bevin's view. The cabinet was informed that the Prime Minister considered that Russia was ready to work with Britain and that, in his judgement, the only real safeguard was agreement between the three Great Powers within the framework of a world organization. Indeed, Churchill went out of his way to cast doubt on the idea of a Western bloc. No immediate threat lay ahead of them once the present war finished, and they should be careful of assuming commitments, consequent upon the formation of a Western bloc, which might impose a heavy military burden upon them.[13] In a private note to Eden, Churchill added that the Allies were hopelessly weak and British policy should be to rely upon sea and air defence.[14]

Attlee, also for strategic reasons, came to another conclusion. Two days after the Armistice and Post-War committee's report on the world organization was completed, Attlee presented to the cabinet a memorandum of his own on 'Foreign Policy and the Flying Bomb'.[15] This threw new light on the Western bloc discussions and, in fact, seems to have been the first paper by any British politician to have addressed itself specifically to the impact of the new weapons on Britain's future strategic situation and, hence, foreign policy. Though the answer to the flying bomb and the rocket had not yet been found, Attlee wrote, it was obvious that Britain could no longer be indifferent to the political position of the countries from which these weapons could be launched. 'We must deny access to the nearer sites and gain space for dealing with those launched at a longer range,' he insisted. There was no choice in the matter; Britain was now 'a continental Power with a vulnerable land frontier'. He went on to claim that events had shown that those who had advocated collective security had been right, that the emergence of the new method of attack by long-range bombardment was conclusive. It followed that they could not afford to have as a buffer between them and a potential enemy a ring of weak neutral states liable to be overrun quickly. They must not only disarm Germany and keep her disarmed, but they must also create a system of defence which would deny to a potential enemy the opportunity of securing bases for launching attacks upon them, and which could furnish positions from which the British could make provision for a counter-attack. In particular, Attlee stated:

> From our point of view, Norway, Denmark, Holland, and France are necessary outposts of Britain and, in as much as Britain is now as she has been for a hundred years a shield for the U.S., outposts of America as well. Their defence is necessary to our defence and without us they cannot defend themselves ... Unless we are prepared to shift the centre of the Commonwealth we must ensure that it is in a strategic position comparable to that of Washington and Moscow. We can only do this by bringing into the closest association with ourselves the countries which hold the keys of our fortress.

Attlee concluded that 'within a general system of collective security there should be a close military alliance between Britain and the States above mentioned'. He, too, did not think that such an organization would be viewed with suspicion by Russia. The *most* 'potential enemy', in Attlee's mind, was still Germany – albeit a disarmed and partitioned Germany. But neither he nor the Foreign Office appear to have realized that if a Western alliance against Germany was logical, so too was an Eastern European alliance. However, no decision about a Western bloc was taken prior to the Yalta or, for that matter, the Potsdam Conference (July–August 1945).

British policy towards Poland, on the other hand, was worked out and remained essentially unchanged in the last six months of 1944, despite the Warsaw situation.* The latter did not, and could not, affect British policy, if for no other reason than that the cabinet was informed from August 28 onwards that all the evidence showed that the Russians were doing their utmost to reach the city.[16] The Polish leader, M. Mikolajczyk, met Attlee on September 10, and was told that the Soviet government had expressed its consent in principle to the landing of

---

* The Polish uprising in Warsaw began on August 1, 1944. Though only a few miles from the city, the Russian advance had exhausted itself – having covered some 300 miles in the previous month. In addition, the Germans had reinforced the Warsaw garrison.

British and American aircraft on Soviet airfields. Mikolajczyk replied that he feared the Soviet government, under technical pretexts, might delay the operation until it was useless. Attlee then stated that such an operation would require the most careful preparations and that these were in progress. This did not satisfy Mikolajczyk and, according to the Polish account,[17] Attlee became markedly impatient. Even had the Russians been willing and able to mount a massive frontal assault on Warsaw, there was no reason to suppose that their political aims would have been deterred by the local Polish insurgents.

Attlee's impatience with the Poles was shared by Churchill; the Prime Minister had told Eden that if Mikolajczyk resigned, no support should be given to his successor. Eden appealed to Bevin to use his influence to get other members of the Polish cabinet to stand by Mikolajczyk. On September 5, Bevin reported that he had done so. He and the other Labour ministers had agreed to do everything possible to strengthen the Polish Prime Minister. But this was to no avail. On November 27, after the resignation of Mikolajczyk and Romer from the Polish government in London, Churchill told the cabinet that there could be no question of breaking off relations, but that they should adopt an attitude of complete detachment and of frigidity and leave the London Poles to look after their own affairs. The less they had to do with them in the way of active relations, the better.[18]

The Polish issue had been thoroughly ventilated previously that month by the cabinet in response to certain direct questions raised by the Polish government. Was the attitude of the British government on the territorial compensation which Poland had been promised in the West so decided that though the United States might not agree to it, the British government would still consider themselves bound to advocate it at the peace settlement? The answer was a categorical 'Yes'. The Poles were also informed that British policy was definitely in favour of extending the Polish frontier up to the line of the Oder, unless Poland, of her own volition, should desire at a later stage a more restricted territorial compensation in the West.

The composition of the future Polish government was a different matter. Here, Churchill said that while agreement might be reached on the frontier, everything might break on the problem of joining forces with the Lublin committee.* This would be a great pity, but the

* The Lublin committee was a group of pro-Soviet Poles set up by the Russians in July 1944 to administer civil affairs in the liberated areas of Poland.

Polish government would be in a much better position on a point of this kind, where they would have the support of Great Britain and probably of the United States, than on the frontier question. Cripps suggested that if a settlement on the frontier question on lines satisfactory to Stalin could be obtained, the differences between the conflicting Polish parties might be resolved if they were linked with the frontier settlement. The Prime Minister had no difficulty in agreeing with this, and it appears to have been the sole contribution of the Labour ministers to the cabinet discussion. It was Sir Archibald Sinclair, the Secretary of State for Air, who pressed Churchill about the position if, after stating that British policy was to extend the Polish frontier to the line of the Oder, negotiations broke down over the composition of the Polish government. Churchill replied that then the representatives of the Polish government in London would return to their country and matters would have to be left to take their own course. In that event the British would stand on the line they had always taken, namely that they would recognize no territorial changes before the peace conference, and that, failing agreement, changes of frontier must be reserved until then. There would be no question of recognizing a government such as the Lublin committee. The cabinet approved the Prime Minister's statement. As for His Majesty's Government guaranteeing the independence and integrity of the new Poland, the cabinet again agreed with Churchill that the policy would be to seek an Anglo-Russian guarantee, with which the United States could subsequently be associated, such a guarantee to last until it could be taken over by the world organization.[19] Moreover, the cabinet's confidence that an agreement – along the lines they had in mind – could be obtained, remained unshaken prior to Yalta.

On January 22, 1945, Bevin optimistically informed his colleagues[20] that, according to reliable sources, M. Gousev's* return to Moscow was due to the desire of the Soviet government to satisfy themselves as to the real trend of opinion in Britain on the Polish issue. Gousev had been told very frankly of the Labour Party's attitude, and it might just be possible that Stalin would be ready to make a dramatic gesture. This might include agreement to the inclusion of Lvov within the boundaries of Poland and the setting-up of a mixed Polish government, possibly including Mikolajczyk and a few other London Poles. It was

---

* Gousev was the Russian Ambassador to Britain and also the Russian representative on the EAC.

said that, if Lvov was given to Poland, Stalin would transfer its population to Russia and build another great Ukrainian city in place of Lvov.... Though these reports could not yet be judged, Bevin argued that if there was anything in them they appeared to constitute an argument against the British coming to any immediate conclusions on the subject. In any case, so far as the eastern frontiers were concerned, Bevin doubted whether there had ever been any real support for the Treaty of Riga,* or any question about the soundness of the Curzon Line save as regards its southern extension – of which he would not himself make a point of principle. Sir Stafford Cripps mentioned the possibility of a joint and several guarantee by the three Great Powers of the independence of Poland, coupled with the constitution of a mixed government and a clear understanding about free elections. The numerous declarations made by Stalin about his anxiety to see Poland live as a free and independent nation would make it very difficult for him to oppose such a solution. Cripps agreed that it would be a mistake, if the Polish situation could be secured in that way, to make the issue of Lvov a stumbling block.

This optimism was somewhat qualified when the cabinet turned to the question of the western Polish boundary. Bevin referred to the suggestions that had been previously made, especially the adoption of the line of the Oder. There was a good deal of criticism in Labour and other circles, he declared, of any such arrangement. It was felt that if the new Poland were to cut so deeply into Pomerania it would be almost impossible for Germany to live at all. It was likely to create an unstable internal position in Poland owing to the size of the German minority that would have to be absorbed, while the problem of transferring the German population of so large an area was, on the face of it, so great as to be almost insoluble. He thought that they would have to be extremely careful how they committed themselves in the matter.

It is not difficult to guess what had prompted these remarks for, a few days afterwards, Bevin indicated his uneasiness at the Bretton Woods proposals,† at least in respect to the details. Sir John Anderson,

---

* An agreement, signed in 1921, between Russia and Poland, by which a common frontier was established.

† These included the creation of an International Monetary Fund and an International Bank for Reconstruction and Development. The preponderance of American financial and economic strength was obvious at the Bretton Woods Conference, which was held in July 1944.

who had become Chancellor of the Exchequer, was at some pains to demonstrate his great sympathy for Bevin's position even though the Chancellor came down on the side of Bretton Woods and the International Monetary Fund.[21] In retrospect, the British economic situation can be envisaged as a time-bomb – the ticking of which, slowly and quietly at first, but with increasing frequency and volume, can be heard as the persistent background noise in all the three 'Great Power'-centred cabinet discussions from now onwards.

Replying to Bevin, Churchill emphasized that they had been careful to avoid any commitment about the western Polish boundary. All they had told the Poles was, if they were prepared to accept the Curzon Line, the British would support them in acquiring, up to the limit of the Oder, as much territory as they could digest. But Churchill indicated that he still thought the difficulty of transferring populations could be overcome. Eden, however, also expressed hesitation about conceding the Oder line and, when the cabinet resumed its discussion of the Polish situation on January 26,[22] he had a memorandum ready which enlarged upon the reasons for his hesitation. It pointed out that the undertaking given to the Polish government in London about the western frontiers had been part of an effort to get the Poles to accept the Curzon Line. Now it seemed probable that the cabinet would have to deal with the Lublin Poles – who accepted the Curzon Line. Thus there was no longer any need to support any more extensive transfers of territory, except that those might be thought fit and proper on other grounds. It was not clear whether the River Neisse meant the eastern or western Neisse. If the latter, the Poles would get practically all Silesia and an additional three million Germans would have to be reckoned with. The present indications were that the Lublin Poles wanted the Oder up to the Görlitzer Neisse – the more westerly tributary. The memorandum suggested that it was time for the British to convey their doubts about this to their Allies – though without prejudging the future settlement. Britain was not committed to supporting anything other than the annexation by Poland of East Prussia, Danzig and the Oppeln district. Churchill and the rest of the cabinet were in complete accord with Eden. The Prime Minister now stated that to remove between 5 and 6 millions was no small matter, but a total figure of 8 or 9 millions would be quite unmanageable. Nor could they be certain that a reduced Germany could absorb so many. Later, he emphasized that the one British bargaining counter was recognition of the Lublin committee as the government of Poland; this was not to be given up except in return for something worth having. In general, he concluded, the British position – if the cabinet agreed – would be to continue to advise the Poles to compromise as regards the eastern frontier, and to remain adamant on the question of ensuring a free, sovereign and independent Poland, coupled with arrangements for free elections.

The cabinet did agree, Morrison adding that there was much sympathy for the Poles among all parties. They were very popular in Britain and there was a good deal of feeling that the Russian attitude towards them had been harsh and imperialist. He hoped they would be able to protect the underground army in Poland from persecution. In view of the cabinet's previous *Realpolitik*, however, it is difficult to imagine that the expression of these sentiments amounted to much more than a verbal face-saving. Notwithstanding the general ideological antagonism towards Soviet Russia and any suspicions about Russian 'imperialism', the British still hoped and even expected to come to some arrangement with the Russians over Poland at Yalta.

The British leaders, including the Labour cabinet ministers, were perfectly aware of what the Polish issue meant to the Russians – besides the fact that there was very little, if anything, they could really do for the Poles. Nor, as yet, was there any fear of Russia; on the contrary, as the Foreign Office had indicated, there was good reason to suppose that co-operation would be in Russia's own interests. Although Poland appeared to be the most urgent item on the Yalta agenda it was not, so far as the British were concerned, the most important one. Germany was still the vital issue, the one for which the war had been fought and, as it later transpired, which had cost the British their empire and jeopardized their entire economic situation in the world. Agreement about Poland was significant mainly as part of a wider arrangement about Germany and, hence, Europe. Even recognition of the Lublin committee was possible, as Churchill had said, 'in return for something worth having'. Poland, as always, was a pawn in the Great Power game, a bargaining counter.

CHAPTER XIII

Towards Potsdam

ALTHOUGH, at the beginning of 1945, the end of 'Hitler's War' was clearly in sight, the magnitude of German power and its continuing ability to withstand the combined onslaught of Britain, the USSR and the United States was almost equally impressive. If some elements in the Labour Party were unhappy about the way the question of Germany's future was apparently being tackled, the Party as a whole had little difficulty in agreeing that this was the single crucial issue in any future peace settlement, so far as Europe was concerned.

True, there were other irritants and in January Greece was the most disturbing of these. Prior to a debate in the Commons on the subject, Greenwood led an NEC delegation – consisting of Laski, Griffiths, Bevan and Morgan Phillips – to Churchill to express the Party's concern at events there. The meeting proved to be a remarkable success for Churchill,[1] though it came rather too late in the day to have any immediate effect on the public furore about Greece, which was not confined to the Labour Party. It proved of very little avail that, in the Commons, the Prime Minister defined the government's policy – in Italy and Yugoslavia as well as Greece – as 'Government of the people, by the people, for the people, set up on a basis of free and universal suffrage election, with secrecy of the ballot and no intimidation'.[2] The Labour opposition had no political option except to continue its public attack, despite its private accord. On a division, the government could find only 340 MPs willing to support it in the lobbies. But this was shadow boxing; the critical amendment was not tabled by a Labour MP but by Sir Richard Acland, leader of the CommonWealth Party. The bulk of the Labour members abstained and the political heat evaporated almost as rapidly as it had developed.

Another, less public irritant was the question of Soviet representation in the United Nations. From the Crimea on February 8, Churchill advised the cabinet that he was now ready to support the reduced

Russian claim for two extra representatives (White Russia and the Ukraine) at the United Nations. He had reached this conclusion on the grounds that Britain would have four or five representatives, that they would derive advantage from not being the only multiple voter, and that it would constitute a friendly gesture to Russia. The cabinet's agreement was not without certain reservations, but they did vouch-safe their majority support. The reservations were in regard to the attitude of the United States President and possible future difficulties about the question of the Dominions. It was stipulated that the Russians would have to protect Britain from subsequent similar claims from any other Soviet socialist republic. Bevin, and the Secretaries for War and the Dominions, were anxious that Churchill should know that, while accepting the cabinet's decision, they were not in agreement with it. The Dominions Secretary was worried about its possible effect on the Dominions, while Bevin and the Secretary for War would have preferred Britain not to commit itself in advance of the United States. Similarly, though reluctant to see Poland receive any lands she might desire east of the Oder – preferring that their allocation should be left to the peace conference – the cabinet also approved Churchill's and Eden's attempt to broaden the base of a new Polish government, and the instant recognition of it, if this could be achieved.

The cabinet's major concern about the Yalta negotiations related to the German question and the two most significant discords about it which occurred at the conference. These were over dismemberment and reparations which, from the British point of view, as Attlee em-phasized, were directly related matters. Regarding the first, Churchill cabled that not only had Stalin pressed strongly for dismemberment, he had received a degree of support from the Americans. The sub-sequent cabinet discussion centred on the meaning of the word, which raised 'great economic and political questions' not so far considered in cabinet nor (save as affecting East Prussia) in the APW committee. It was thus desirable to avoid any commitment until the subject had been considered. The cabinet discussion on the second issue appears to have been even more lengthy. Attlee summarized the 'general sense' of the cabinet as follows:

(1) Reparations must be considered together with, and as part of, any policy of dismemberment.
(2) The two objects which the Russians had in view, the depletion

of the manufacturing capacity of Germany, and the preservation of her ability to make large annual reparation payments, were essentially incompatible with each other. The wise course, and the one Great Britain should concentrate on, would be the maximum withdrawal from the German potential over a period of, say, two years. The history of what had happened regarding reparations at the end of the last war, and the possibility that the United States might, at a relatively early date, cease to participate in the occupation of Germany, were strong arguments for ensuring that anything that Britain was to secure should be secured in the first two years after the war.

(3) While it might be possible for the USSR and other allies to absorb deliveries of manufactured goods from current production, Britain's own economic situation would only permit the acceptance of certain raw materials.

(4) It had to be decided whether or not it was desirable that Germany should continue to have an economic life in the future. The criterion of what machinery, equipment, etc. to remove from Germany should be its value, or the value of the industry which it served, for war potential. Britain should concentrate on removing material of this kind, together with overseas investments.

(5) Britain was more concerned than the United States or the USSR with the future of Europe, and the creation of a decent Europe was one of the war aims.

(6) The British should oppose the Russian idea of a priority class of powers, consisting of the United States, the USSR and Britain, to receive reparations, while the balance was left for division among the smaller Allies.

(7) Britain should agree to the setting up of a committee to work out the application of the principles governing the extraction and division of reparations, and should see that France and the smaller allies were associated with this committee.*[3]

The war cabinet approved Attlee's summary and invited him to submit a revised draft for their consideration. This, with minor amendments, was despatched to Churchill on February 9.[4] The note stressed two

* This material is reproduced by permission of the Controller of Her Majesty's Stationery Office.

other points, that no figures could be quoted without further investigation but that, anyhow, the Russian figures were far too high, and that Britain had to avoid the risk of having to pay for the imports necessary to keep Germany alive while other powers received reparations from her.

The results of the Yalta Conference, Attlee pronounced to the cabinet, were highly satisfactory.[5] Agreement had been reached on the United States' proposals for the Dumbarton Oaks Constitution; agreement had been reached on Poland, and the Prime Minister and Foreign Secretary had succeeded in keeping the question of the new western frontiers open; the principle of dismemberment had been agreed, but ample elbow-room had been retained; similarly, the principle of reparations had been accepted, and the Moscow Reparations Commission established to consider the amount and the methods; France had been invited to receive a zone of Germany (to be taken from the British and American zones) and a seat on the Allied Control Commission. There had been no dispute as to the necessity of measures for the denazification, demilitarization and disarmament of Germany. The cabinet expressed its great satisfaction at Attlee's review of these results, and invited him to send a telegram of congratulation to the Prime Minister and the Foreign Secretary, which he did.

The Labour ministers had particular cause for this initial satisfaction with the Yalta results. In the first place there was the continuing involvement of the United States and the inclusion of France in the German settlement. Secondly, there appeared to be a reasonable possibility of more general agreement along the lines that they, notably Attlee, had been advocating. The approach of the end of the war had brought no fundamental change either to their attitude or policy regarding Germany, though there was a certain shift in emphasis* which was primarily due to a greater awareness of the economic problem. Bevin cautioned a gathering of the World Trades Union Conference, in February, that while there was no reason to be 'soft'

---

* Curiously enough, this shift coincided with the accidental deaths during the year of two prominent Labour Party 'hard-liners' on Germany, A. J. Dobbs and James Walker. Little significance is to be attached to this, though an odd parallel with the earlier demise of George Lansbury – which had symbolized the decline of pacifist influence – may be noted. More important, probably, was the elimination of Gillies, as this was deliberate. The International sub-committee of the NEC (with both Attlee and Morrison present) decided unanimously in January that the Party's International Department needed a new Secretary, and Gillies was told to resign.[6]

with Germans – they would have to go a long way in making reparations – the Labour movement would have to be very careful in working
out the methods of its approach to this aspect of the settlement. It
would be only too easy to make sixty million people in the centre of
Europe a submerged labour force which, if not handled correctly,
could bring down the standards of all other countries.[7] Greenwood
said much the same thing in the Commons; 'no nation', he warned,
'could profit by the more or less permanent impoverishment of sixty
or eighty million European people.'[8] The *Daily Herald* added that
perpetual policemanship was an unthinkable prospect and that every
effort should be made to ensure the development of a genuine German
democracy.[9]

The predominant attitude towards Germany, both in the cabinet
and Labour Party, remained a severe one. A speech made by Cripps
in January, suggesting that only God could judge the Germans,[10]
became the subject of a special meeting of the war cabinet a few days
afterwards.[11] Privately, as will shortly be seen, Cripps took a rather
different position. Attlee made his own view quite clear in public: 'If
you ask,' he said in the Commons during the Yalta debate, 'who is
responsible for the movements [of population], this terrible thing that
has smitten Europe, there is no doubt at all that it is the Nazi rulers of
Germany and the people of Germany who actively supported them.'
He did not suggest that an indictment could be drawn against a whole
people, but neither could a whole people be relieved of responsibility.
A great many of the German people had accepted Nazi ideas.

> They have broken down the old barriers, and therefore I say that
> they cannot appeal to the old Europe. If they have to yield, to make
> restoration, they are not entitled to appeal on the basis of the moral
> laws that they have disregarded or the pity and mercy that they
> have never extended to any others.

Though he did not believe in treating them as they had treated others,
they would have no right to complain if pieces of their territory were
given to the Dutch or Poles. The central problem of Europe was that
of the German people. It was idle to think that the process of converting
the Germans from the barbarities into which they had sunk to civilization was not going to take a long time. . . .[12]

The Yalta agreements were not unattended by domestic political
difficulties, but these were largely confined to the Polish question and

to Conservative rebels. Churchill, against Attlee's advice,[13] insisted on making the entire Yalta declaration the subject of a vote of confidence. The Prime Minister's view was that the Conference had faced difficulties and realities in an exceptional manner. He eventually obtained his vote, by 413 votes to 0, but not before an amendment was laid before the House regretting 'the decision to transfer to another power the territory of an ally contrary to the Atlantic Charter . . .' and also the failure to ensure that the liberated nations had the right to choose their own governments . . . Stokes voted for this amendment, but Bevan and the other Left-wingers supported the government, which won by 396 votes to 25. On the main motion, moreover, Greenwood, speaking for the official opposition, announced his general support: his main criticism was in regard to Poland.[14] The Poles, he considered, had not been sufficiently consulted over what was going to happen to Poland. Here, Bevan and the Left, as well as Stokes, abstained. But this manoeuvring could not, and did not, obscure the fact that for Labour as a whole, the crux of the Yalta Conference was Germany.

The Left continued to view the problem in a quite different fashion from the Party hierarchy. The unconditional surrender policy, vigorously re-affirmed in public by Churchill in January, was condemned almost up to the very moment of the German collapse.[15] The absence of any detailed plans for Germany, coupled with General Eisenhower's 'no-fraternization' order, was held responsible by the *New Statesman* for the fear which was moving the Germans to their last ditch desperation. The Germans, the paper explained, were afraid that the Allies' deep-rooted suspicion of each other would allow Germany to lapse through inaction 'into a ruined no-man's-land in which no wheel turns, there are no wages or bread, and pestilence marches with the underground gunmen'.[16] Answering his own question, 'How Do We Keep Germany Disarmed?', Bevan derided any notion of doing this by means of impoverishment or dismemberment. Those methods ignored all the social and political causes of war in the modern world and served merely to convert Germany 'from a problem into an obsession'. There was no surer recipe for bringing about a German national revival. The important question was whether the need for security against German military resurgence would be regarded by the victorious Powers as an excuse for national ambitions or as a secular task. If the latter, then the task was simple. The factory inspector, the agent of civilization at home, could solve the problem of security abroad. To base the post-war international unity on an alliance to prevent the rise of Germany was 'to substitute a mania for a policy'.[17]

Before the end of March 1945, the ticking of the economic time-bomb had become more audible; the Chancellor of the Exchequer warned the cabinet that reparations and dismemberment ought to be seen as alternative policies. Reparations on the scale that the Russians were demanding could only be obtained if Germany was treated as an economic whole.[18] The Labour ministers adhered, nevertheless, to their German policy; Churchill and Eden also were not inclined to take the Chancellor's arguments as decisively as the historian, Sir Llewellyn Woodward has claimed.[19] It was decided to continue the procedure established at Yalta, of having two separate bodies to study the issue, though instructions given to the British representatives on both bodies might be considered together. The cabinet, Churchill concluded,[20] would have to look at the question again later, but this task was undertaken neither by the Coalition nor by the caretaker government which succeeded it. Relations with the Russians deteriorated shortly after the cabinet meeting and a new complexion was given to the entire situation by the Russian intimation that they were reconsidering their views on dismemberment.*

Evidence of the extent to which the Labour ministers were prepared to support their German policy was not slow in forthcoming. Towards the end of April, Attlee presented a memorandum to the cabinet indicating that the APW committee favoured the continuation of some form of compulsory military service after the war. The Labour ministers merely wanted, said Bevin, to consult responsible members of their Party and the TUC before any public announcement was made. They were confident that the support of the Labour movement would be obtained. The cabinet readily endorsed the APW committee's decision and agreed to the Labour ministers' request.[21] The agreement of the NEC[22] and the general council of the TUC was, subsequently, secured. There could be no doubt of the Labour hierarchy's determination.

In April also, the APW committee discussed Eden's long-promised but essentially inconclusive paper on dismemberment. The Secretary for War, Sir James Grigg, speculated that they might be presented

---

* Stalin formally announced that the Russians did not intend to dismember Germany on May 9, 1945.

with a *de facto* dismemberment of Germany whether they liked it or not. Attlee pointed out that the committee had all along favoured some degree of decentralization.[23] It was decided to send Eden's paper to the economic and industrial staff for comment. With Bevin in the chair, the APW committee met on May 10, to consider three other papers. The first of these was a report by the same experts, namely the Economic and Industrial Planning Staff (EIPS), containing specific proposals about the German industries to be restricted and the type of restrictions to be imposed. The report was based on the APW committee's previous decision that the policy in the field of economic security should be to apply draconian measures to a selected field of German industry, leaving the rest more or less undisturbed. The second paper to be discussed was a memorandum by A. V. Alexander suggesting that the above proposals, which included the prohibition, for the period of occupation only, of German building and ownership of ocean-going ships, were inadequate and that British policy should be to effect the total and permanent elimination of the German shipbuilding and shipping industries. This, he argued, was necessary and possible within the APW policy for draconian measures in selected industries. The third paper came from Cripps and it, besides assuming the elimination of the German aircraft industry, also urged a drastic reduction in the German engineering industry, at any rate during the occupation.[24]

The committee members prefaced their discussion by agreeing with Bevin that economic measures against Germany for the purpose of security should henceforth be described as the 'disarmament of German industrial war potential'. They further agreed that the first priority for policy decisions should be that of security – which Bevin and Cripps strongly advocated. Cripps then boldly declared that he did not think that the neutralization of Germany's industrial war potential could be achieved by the elimination or restriction of a few selected industries. Alexander argued that 'many of our Allies have the same interests as ourselves, in preventing both a future threat to sea communications and German industrial competition'. Bevin, however, suggested that the committee should get on with its arranged agenda – deciding which industries should be eliminated or restricted – and this was accepted.

The EIPS's report proposed measures of restrictions in two categories: (*a*) those on which a decision in principle should be taken immediately, and (*b*) those industries on which a decision should be deferred pending an on-the-spot examination. Merchant shipping figured in the first of these categories and for its prohibition during the occupation period was substituted the phrase 'until further notice'. Regarding steel, it was agreed that reduction in capacity should be to about fifty per cent of the 'pre-war capacity' and there should be no restoration of any capacity destroyed or damaged during the war. Moreover, imports of high-grade ore could be controlled by the Allies. It was agreed that ammonia, which was essential for manufacture of fertilizers for food production, should not be eliminated until the Control Commission recommended that its production in Germany was no longer essential. No other postponement in this first category could be allowed and the committee's decisions here may be summarized as follows:

Industry	Duration of prohibition
Civil aircraft	Indefinite
Merchant shipping and shipbuilding	As amended
Steel	Occupation period
Machine tools	Occupation period
Ball and roller bearings	Occupation period
Synthetic oil	Indefinite
Ammonia and methanol	Indefinite

In spite of the fact that, in Churchill's words, 'less cordial relations had developed with Russia since the Yalta Conference',[25] the last meetings of the Coalition government's Armistice and Post-War committee thus provide clear evidence that policy towards Germany remained almost unaffected. One way or another, the latter's power to make war on her own was to be decisively reduced. Certain differences as to how this might be achieved did not obscure the overall agreement, which transcended Party lines, that it was to be achieved. The Labour ministers, in particular, were firmly resolved that the second German war would be the final one. A further indication of the prevailing collective cabinet mood in April 1945 may be gathered from its rejection of a proposal by the War Crimes Commission for an inter-Allied criminal court. The appropriate tribunal, it was felt, would be a military tribunal. A special procedure should be devised for leaders and active members of the Gestapo or the SS, by which a mixed military tribunal would be invited to find that members of these organizations had been engaged in a criminal conspiracy, etc. When this general judgement had been given, any such person could be charged with being a member of this criminal conspiracy, and punished accordingly.[26] Or, in other words, the British intended to shoot them.*

After the Yalta declaration, the Labour Left continued its criticism of Allied policy on Germany. The Allies had plenty of slogans about punishment, wrote the *New Statesman*, but where was their constructive policy? The paper attributed the greater part of the blame to Britain and the United States. The very idea of even minimal rehabilitation of Germany was taboo, the *New Statesman* believed, because these governments feared to arouse Russian suspicions of Western tenderness to Germans. The Russians were realists, however; they wanted peace terms which would provide, above all, for the security of the Soviet Union. The *New Statesman* urged that the administration of Germany, in the first instance, be carried on by joint Allied teams of practical men.[27] *Tribune* on the other hand, was as doubtful of Russian 'realism' as that of the West. The Communists, in fact, were now among the enthusiastic supporters of the division of zones of influence between the Allies. 'They have, as it were, replaced the old watchword "Workers of the World, Unite!" by a new one: "Workers of the World, divide into three zones!".' But neither the working classes in Europe nor even perhaps the working class in Russia would benefit from this in the long run. The Left supporters of Teheran (and Yalta) seemed definitely to have written off Germany as a possible factor in the Labour movement in Europe after the war, yet there could be no renaissance of the European Labour movement without a re-birth of German Socialism. This was not likely to happen if the German working classes were to be made responsible and punished for the criminal excesses of the Nazis. *Tribune* feared that the interests and the power of Labour in Europe were being sacrificed to a highly unstable diplomatic conception. 'Revolution from above' in Eastern Europe could well prove to be abortive and, at the same time, the paper did not see why the interests of Western European Labour should be disregarded.[28]

Western European Socialists, however, had their own difficulties in regard to the problem of Germany – notably a disagreement between the British Labour Party and the French Socialists. The question of Anglo-French relations had been taken up by the Labour Party's

---

* This was an initial view. It was later changed in view of certain objections by the United States and the USSR, the death of Hitler and by the burden that would be placed on military tribunals.

advisory committee on International Affairs shortly after the 1944 annual conference. A report was drawn up in December but, as the result of an International Socialist conference held at Transport House in early March 1945, it had to be revised. Dalton presided at this conference and, much to his surprise, found that the French delegation were for 'an extremely mild approach' towards the German problem. He therefore informed them 'very firmly that the British Labour Party could not agree to a declaration against dismemberment'.[29] The revised report[30] stressed that a satisfactory Franco-British relationship should be the cornerstone of the Labour Party's European policy, whatever the general policy of the Party. While it was true that Labour ought not to allow the German problem to dominate their thinking, they would be very fortunate indeed if any effective international organization could be made to function for some years following the armistice. If this were due to Big Power disagreement, then 'the German problem [would] inevitably dominate our international thinking', unless a positive alternative could be offered. A closely related Britain and France would form a basis for the latter and would be able 'in the immediate post-war years to give Europe that feeling of immediate military security which is essential for the future working out of international relations'. However, the revised report glossed over the actual impasse that had been reached.

It is probable that his knowledge of this report provides the true explanation of a famous and often misquoted remark by Bevin at the Labour Party's 1945 annual conference, in May. 'France was [*sic*] going Left,' he predicted, 'and Left understands Left, but Right does not.'[31] Bevin reiterated that while Germany had to be prevented from developing a war potential, sixty to eighty million people could not be left derelict. The Germans had to grow food because neither the United States nor Britain could feed them, however sentimental they might be. German p.o.w.s had to be returned to their zones in order to till the soil but, noting that German industry had raised its war potential by sixty per cent under the Hitler régime, Bevin insisted that this part of industry would have to be controlled and eliminated so that the Germans could not constitute a danger again. Yet Bevin could not have succeeded in bridging the two national schools of opinion any more than he could have closed the gap within his own party. On the subject of Germany both Attlee and Bevin were now much less inclined to propose courses of action in public which might later prove precipitate; but it was only in this respect that they differed from Dalton.

The two Labour cabinet ministers, however, had become very much more aware, and perhaps fearful, of the underlying difficulties in the general international situation as the end of the war approached. As a result, they had both, during February and March, gone on record as favouring not only party solidarity regarding foreign policy but also national solidarity. Attlee began his speech on the Yalta debate by emphasizing that foreign policy decisions were war cabinet decisions – though, of course, in view of the discontent of a number of Conservative MPs at the time, this remark also had a party edge to it. More positively, he concluded by saying that he wanted to think that the acceptance of the vote of confidence motion would be a step towards 'the achievement of a unity of policy in foreign affairs and defence...'.[32] In March, Bevin referred to the 'imperative necessity for the will of the nation as a whole to be expressed, and for a combined effort to be made'.[33] This note was partly due to awareness of British economic weakness and partly to a realization of the extent to which the achievement of any British policy would depend upon American support, still an uncertain factor. It was also due to anxiety over Russian policy. Upon his return from San Francisco, where he had attended the United Nations conference with Eden (an action denounced by *Tribune* as his 'Crowning Blunder'[34]), Attlee told Dalton that the Russians were 'behaving in a perfectly bloody way, telling us nothing, but setting up Puppet Governments all over Europe as far west as they could'.[35]

It was on this point that Dalton significantly diverged from Attlee and Bevin. The latter were, if anything, even more ideologically antagonistic towards the country which, to them, epitomized totalitarian communism than was Churchill – though Bevin, like the Prime Minister, hoped or believed that a favourable deal might be arranged with Stalin, provided United States support could be secured. Attlee, it seems clear, never really thought this a serious possibility. Dalton's views here may well have been an additional factor in Attlee's selection of Bevin as Foreign Secretary when Labour took office. Dalton told Attlee privately that, if made Foreign Secretary, he could probably come as near to understanding and dealing with the Russians as anybody, being sure that they had to be met with both strength and understanding, a combination that he was not confident was then the case.[36] Attlee was almost certainly sceptical of this claim – he avoided any direct response to it – and perhaps transferred some of his scepticism to Dalton himself after Dalton's public statement at the Party conference. Almost alone among the leadership, Dalton was bold enough to assert that:

> Given that Anglo-Soviet relations are still clouded from time to time by suspicion and misunderstanding, I most emphatically hold that a British Labour Government is far more likely to remove these suspicions than a British Tory Government.[37]

'I have heard speeches,' Attlee remarked, 'that suggested that all international problems could be solved if we could only get a few people sitting around the table and discussing them. Believe me, the thing is not as easy as that.'[38]

The usual conflicting opinions were to be heard at the conference. Ellen Wilkinson, the chairman, said that they would have to do things in Germany that they hated to do because they had to bring home to the Germans the fact that a nation was responsible for its government. From the floor a resolution was moved calling for the punishment of war criminals, de-nazification, disarmament, international control of heavy industry, socialization of Junker estates, and the restoration of German democratic political, trade-union and co-operative institutions. Another resolution advocated the full use of Socialist refugee teachers in Germany. There was some criticism that Attlee had not been Socialist, or Socialist enough, in his analysis of the European situation. Other speakers insisted again on distinguishing between Nazis and Germans.

It was Bevin, in the course of his reply to the International debate on behalf of the executive, who scored the most noteworthy oratorical and Party success. Foreign affairs, he pronounced, were different from domestic affairs, in that they could settle the latter among themselves, whereas the former constituted 'the most vexed and difficult problem' which would confront a future Labour government. Prejudices and economic differences could not be easily resolved; even revolutions did not change geography and geographical needs. Nor could agreement over a peace be brought by slogans, as wars were caused by a combination of factors. What the Labour ministers in the Coalition had tried to do, Bevin stated, was to stress the importance of economic problems. Europe would become 'a cesspool of disease' unless great care was taken, he warned. He went out of his way to emphasize Labour's desire for good relations with Russia; while they wanted

both eastern and western European States to have freely elected governments, he pledged that a Labour government would never use the
small states as instruments against the big states.[39] Bevin's speech
effectively concluded the 1945 conference's deliberations on international affairs. Attlee and Bevin were thus enabled to attend the
Potsdam and subsequent international conferences during the year,
with virtually free hands so far as the Party was officially concerned.

CHAPTER XIV

Conclusions

THIS book has argued that the British Labour Party, through its leaders in the war cabinet, played a major role in the formulation of British foreign policy during the Second World War. Churchill's use of 'personal diplomacy', somewhat romanticized by his own historical account of it, has tended to obscure the fact that British policy was a Coalition policy. Yet the very existence of the government originally depended upon an effective political partnership between Churchill's rebel Tories and the Labour Party. The partnership came into being because its principals were committed to a policy of absolute resistance to Nazi Germany. Although the military and political character of the war changed dramatically, the key issue for the British government, which subsumed that of all others, remained that of Germany. It was precisely in this area that the contributions of the Labour ministers were of particular importance.

In the course of the war the Labour Party's 'ideological' approach shifted considerably: the question of Germany became, in effect, the German question. This led to a Labour, and British, European policy which had, as its principal object, a decisive and permanent reduction in German power. Germany alone was never again to be in a position to threaten the security of Europe. The combined efforts of Attlee and Bevin, as well as those of other Labour ministers, were directed towards ensuring that the method by which this aim was to be achieved would be thorough enough. There can be little doubt that though the exact nature of these efforts was largely unknown to most members of the Labour Party at the time, their general tendency fully accorded with official Party policy.

This is significant because it was the 'German question' which most engaged the Party ideologically and on which most Labour dissent was focused. It was the sole issue upon which all Party dissentients were entirely agreed. It was not only a vital matter of practical politics but also a moral question, deeply rooted in Labour principles. As such it became the leading issue of Party controversy during the war, giving rise to a sustained, though essentially fruitless, attempt to change official policy. This study, therefore, has also been concerned to demonstrate the way in which the Labour Party responded to, and resolved, the dispute.

At the beginning of the war few questions appeared less controversial than that of Labour's attitude to Germany. What, above all, united the Party was the conviction that the British ultimatum represented a challenge not to Germany *per se* but to the Nazi government of that country. All factions, including the pacifists, had utterly condemned fascism; at the same time the Labour Party had always been critical of the Versailles settlement. In September 1939, there was virtually unanimous agreement that a fundamental distinction had to be made between the Nazi Party and the German people as a whole. However, there was also very general agreement – with the exception of the pacifists – that the German invasion of Poland constituted a clear *casus belli*.

More particularly, the belated decision of the Chamberlain government to 'resist' Hitler was viewed as the replacement of the government's own foreign policy with that of Labour's. This, in turn, brought about a very great revival of Party confidence. Labour, with much justification, could and did claim to 'speak for England'. Greenwood, significantly, referred to the nation's honour; the original draft of *Labour, the War and the Peace* included a section headed 'Britain's Historic Task'. The advent of the war also emphasized the national importance of Labour's extra-parliamentary strength. The Party as a whole regained a new sense of purpose; even the Left wing was momentarily encouraged.

Yet it was not long before certain elements in the Party began to have second thoughts. There was a danger, they considered, that the conflict might develop into something other than an anti-fascist struggle. This idea was reinforced by the position of the Soviet Union, the continued existence of the Chamberlain government, and the unexpected nature of the 'war's' first developments. Also, the old fear of the consequences of an all-out war re-asserted itself to some degree, especially among what might be called the intellectual Left. The pacifists, moreover, continued to hope for a negotiated peace and, in Richard Stokes, found a new, energetic leader. The result was a two-fold demand – for a change in the government, and for a clear statement of war or peace aims.

The Party's leadership, initially, resisted both demands. Nothing could be done about the former and, while the political wing had some sympathy for the second, the industrial wing had not. The Royal Navy and the French army were still intact and thus the Labour leaders were content, despite the elimination of Poland, to rest on their position that there could be no treating of any sort with the Nazis but, equally, continuing to distinguish between the latter and the German people.

There existed, however, divergent views in both the hierarchy and dissentient factions of the Party. Dalton had viewed the war from the beginning in nationalist as well as ideological terms. For him, its purpose was clear – the elimination of the Nazis and a decisive reduction in German power. On the other hand, people such as Bevan and Zilliacus, were also certain that the war would have to be fought in some fashion, but insisted that its aim would have to be the eradication of the causes of fascism. Bevan, in this respect, tended to emphasize the necessity for radical social and economic changes at home, Zilliacus, the opportunity that the war presented for aiding and encouraging revolutions abroad.

The most important effect of the Soviet attack on Finland was to intensify nationalistic sentiment within the Party. It also strengthened the hierarchy's general antagonism towards and suspicion of all totalitarian régimes, though the Party did not lose sight of the fact that the most immediate danger came from Nazi Germany. In February 1940, Labour made it clear that it aimed at 'total victory' over the latter. The empirical approach contained in the 'doctrine' of 'the lesser evil' which was then enunciated, subscribed to by Laski himself, 'ideologically' facilitated the Party's subsequent entry into the Coalition government led by Winston Churchill. Having made its choice of ideological priorities, the leadership henceforth was prepared to take a profoundly pragmatic view of the domestic political situation and also of the political and military strategies to be pursued.

When Hitler turned towards the West the intellectual Left conceded that the war would have to be fought. Indeed, the Coalition was warmly and widely welcomed by the Party as a whole, despite the new government's retention of most of the 'Men of Munich'. The military crisis, the government's initial domestic actions and the appointment of Cripps as Ambassador to Moscow all contributed to this reception. But what counted most for Labour was the emotional posture of the new government, which was one of exalted patriotism.

There was, however, rather more to the political nature of the Coalition than that. Apart from the defeat of Germany, the Labour ministers made it clear during the war that they strongly shared certain other views on foreign policy with their Coalition colleagues. Attlee indicated his aim of involving the United States in the European peace settlement in November 1941. By January 1942, both Attlee and Bevin had emphatically demonstrated their basic distrust of Soviet ambitions in Eastern Europe. All the Labour ministers were always agreed on the necessity for the re-creation of a strong France. And, perhaps most important for Coalition policy, Attlee revealed that Labour supported the post-war maintenance of some form of imperial or Commonwealth association. It would hardly be much of an exaggeration to assert that it was Churchill and the Conservative rebels who joined Labour quite as much as the reverse. Labour helped to develop policies which in the past might have been described as traditionally British rather than traditionally socialist.

British war strategy, in the first instance, owed little to political considerations, being largely dictated by German military successes. The primary question was one of survival. Attlee and Dalton toyed for a while with the possibility of encouraging a German revolution – Dalton having a government responsibility for seeing what might be done in this direction. But Attlee acquiesced fairly readily to Churchill's opposition to what was thought to be an essential component of such a tactic, namely a further clarification of British war aims. The Coalition itself was more politically vulnerable than the Nazi government. The consideration may also have existed that, should a revolution have taken place in Germany, the British would have been freer (in the absence of specific aims) to negotiate with whatever German régime replaced that of Hitler. There was the possibility, as well, that a British government may have been forced to come to terms with Nazi Germany.

Even the transformation of the war, in the second half of 1941, made no immediate impact on British plans for winning it, as there were no such plans. The government, instead, remained clear as to how the war might be lost, which led to a strategy the essence of which was the avoidance of any direct Anglo-German military confrontation.

Therefore, by early 1942, two broad strategic decisions – with far-reaching political implications – were made. The first, in conjunction with the Americans, was that Germany was so powerful in relation to Japan that it had to be 'Germany first'. The second unilateral decision, to which the Americans subscribed only after very great efforts by Churchill, was that any intervention in force on the Continent would only take place after the Germans had been decisively weakened by previous failure against Russia. (This, of course, was always supposing that the Russians managed to withstand the original German offensive.) The political effects of these decisions became apparent in 1943, the year in which the direct influence of the Labour ministers over foreign policy matters grew considerably. By then the change in Labour's official approach to the 'German question' had manifested itself – with the concomitant war aim of a permanent reduction in German power.

Apart from military defeat and a resulting political and social purge, Attlee and Bevin considered that this aim would best be achieved if (a) the central German governmental machine were completely destroyed, and (b) if Germany were dismembered. Bevin went even further than Attlee at times, and spoke of a return to the days of Bismarck. Attlee was content to work for a truncated Germany, plus a three- or four-way division of the rump which, he suspected, might easily become the basis of a more permanent solution. Both Labour leaders agreed that British interests necessitated British occupation (and therefore control) of the industrial north-western zone, and also that major reparations would have to be made.

On the other hand, the limits of their German policy should also be emphasized. The Labour leaders were aware that it would not be in British interests to create chaos in Germany and they did not intend this. They were prepared to run certain risks in this direction, though these became increasingly circumscribed as the extent of Britain's own economic predicament became known.

These views were in full accord with official statements of Party policy. The man most responsible for such statements was Dalton, an extremist on the issue. Laski, with the able support of Noel-Baker, had some success in toning down the more extreme expressions of anti-German sentiment but, from 1943 onwards, there could be little doubt of its strength, particularly in trade-union circles. The lobbying by Gillies and the 'Fight For Freedom' group was probably more influential than that by Stokes and the 'Peace Aimers' though, owing to tactical mistakes, each tended to be counter-productive. Dalton was allowed plenty of room in which to manœuvre – of which he took maximum advantage – but the mood of the Party was anyway receptive to his approach.

Whether Churchill quite expected that Attlee, as chairman of all the more important committees of the war cabinet dealing with the post-war settlement, would have had as much influence as he did have, is a moot point. It is possible, perhaps probable, that the Prime Minister privately hoped or expected to shape the broad outlines of the peace by means of 'personal diplomacy'. If so he was disappointed during the war as well as after it. Indeed, by downgrading the influence of the Foreign Office, Churchill enhanced the influence of the cabinet committees. The Foreign Secretary was obliged to argue his case on an equal footing with the chiefs of staff and other ministers. Attlee and Bevin had every opportunity to represent Labour's views.

Everyone was aware that British policy for Germany was fraught with significance for Anglo-Soviet relations. Cripps, Dalton and Morrison were the first Labour ministers to think in terms of the possibility of an Anglo-American-Russian peace settlement. Bevin came round forcibly to this idea, via a 'realistic' world organization in 1944, but Attlee appears to have been consistently sceptical, though willing to attempt it. Attlee was rather more favourable to ideas that appeared to him more likely of attainment, such as those of a Western bloc and a divided Germany. In the light of hindsight it is difficult to deny that he was right.

But where Attlee, and especially the Foreign Office, erred was in supposing that the creation of a Western bloc would not inevitably, sooner or later, involve the addition in part or whole of Germany. The chiefs of staff were quite clear on this – a Western bloc without at least western Germany would not provide the solution to the future defence problem of Britain, even if underwritten by the United States. Although neither Attlee nor the Labour hierarchy had any ideological sympathy for Stalinist Russia – quite the contrary, the basis of their European policy was anti-German rather than anti-Russian. Attlee's concept of a Western bloc at most represented an insurance policy – against German resurgence, Russian predominance and American withdrawal. He may not have considered sufficiently the fact that if a Western alliance against Germany were necessary, so too might it be thought that an Eastern alliance was necessary. This could have been because Labour's German policy was, in one respect, so obviously to Russia's long-term advantage. A decisively weakened Germany meant Russian predominance in Eastern Europe which, indeed, was the clear result of the war. It was, however, to counterbalance this that Attlee, and every other cabinet minister for that matter, hoped that the United States would participate actively in the peace settlement – but nobody could be certain. . . .

So intense was the moral heat generated by the Party friction on the issue of German guilt and British policy towards Germany that the above and other aspects of European policy received far less attention by the Party as a whole than might otherwise have been the case. Stokes's position was a singular one; for him the real and most dangerous enemy was the Soviet Union. The *New Statesman* group was always inclined to take a sympathetic view of Soviet policy, not so much from ideological empathy as from what was considered to have happened internationally in the 1930s, and from what was considered realistic in the circumstances of the war. G. D. H. Cole, Harold Laski and Kingsley Martin, for instance, were neither fellow-travellers nor 'communists'. But they did believe that social and political upheavals in Europe, particularly Eastern Europe, were both desirable and inevitable. *Tribune* and notably Bevan, on the other hand, became disenchanted with both Soviet and Western policy and, at the end of the war occupied a position of almost splendid isolation, perhaps rivalled only by people such as H. N. Brailsford.

All the Labour dissentients, however, argued that a 'harsh' post-war policy towards Germany would simply repeat the 'errors' of the previous war's peace settlement, would precipitate, that is, a return to 'power politics' and international anarchy. In other respects the Labour Left was continually obliged to modify, sometimes radically, many of its more particular views of the politics of the war at the time. Instances here include the Second Front, India, Italy (at least after Russia's approval) and even, privately, in regard to Greece.

For the Left, the war brought one ideological disillusionment after another. There were the initial shocks caused by the Soviet Union's pact with Nazi Germany, its share in the partition of Poland and its attack on Finland. There was the crushing of the widespread hope that a revolution might occur in Germany. There was what was called the 'phoney peace', replete with 'power-politics' and barely veiled disagreement. Perhaps the unkindest cut of all, emotionally, was the

Conclusions

emergence of a 'nationalist' and, by 1945, even an 'imperialist' tendency in Labour Party thinking.

And yet, it was the German issue on which all the factions of the Left, as well as the other Labour critics, proved most and, indeed, completely unyielding. Unconditional surrender was unreservedly condemned, as were any notions of dismemberment or of punishing the German people as a whole. This was always the central historical and ideological issue of the entire war. It was here that the Left held firm despite the erosion of its principles in other areas and, perhaps most ironically, despite the fact that it was in this area where criticism could accomplish least.

It may be noted, however, that Bevan was the most consistent and plausible of the Labour wartime critics, though it was his criticism of issues other than that of the German issue which made him plausible. In particular, it may well be that it was his criticism of Soviet policy – which led to his advocacy of a Western bloc (though without the United States) – which subsequently ensured his political advancement. Laski was equally ineffective during the war, except for his part in moderating official statements on German policy. But Laski was considerably more irritating to the Party's hierarchy, not only for what was considered his irresponsible use of his position on the NEC, but also because of his views about Russian policy. His spectacular intervention in the general election served merely to emphasize the essential agreement on foreign policy between the Labour Party and Churchill; it certainly ended any remaining influence that Laski may have possessed.

The successful termination of the military aspect of the European war did not reconcile the Left either to its political results or to the Party's official pronouncement on the International Post-War Settlement. The defeat of Germany, commented the New Statesman, was only the beginning of a struggle to rid the world for ever of the economic and political circumstances in which Hitlerism had been cradled. The peace had not been prepared, and the result was deplorable. 'We began with a phoney war,' wrote V. S. Pritchett, 'we return to a phoney peace, or peace on the instalment plan.'[1] The Labour ministers took their seats at the second and most important half of the Potsdam Conference in an altogether different mood. A British official who was present noted the 'strangely Hanoverian atmosphere ... contrasting with the gay régime of the Stuarts. They are very businesslike and imperturbable, these new people, and give confidence to all around them.'[2] This is understandable for if – so far as popular British belief was concerned – it had been Churchill's War, then it was – in reality – Labour's Peace, one for which the foundations had been laid by Attlee and Bevin during the war itself.

Notes

The following abbreviations have been used: CAB – *Cabinet Papers*; PREM – *Prime Minister's Office Papers*; HC Deb. – *House of Commons, Parliamentary Debates*; Attlee, *Papers (U.)* – *C. R. Attlee Papers, University College, Oxford*; LPCR – *Labour Party, Reports of the Annual Conference*; TUC, Ann. Report – *Trades Union Congress, Reports of the Proceedings of the Annual Conference*; NEC, Minutes – *National Executive Committee of the Labour Party, Minutes of Meetings*.

INTRODUCTION

1. C. F. Brand, *The British Labour Party: A Short History* (Stanford, California, 1964), 227.
2. P. Stansky ed., *The Left and War: The British Labour Party and World War I* (New York, 1969), 4.
3. See, C. A. Cline, *Recruits To Labour: The British Labour Party, 1914–31* (Syracuse, New York, 1963).
4. J. F. Naylor, *Labour's International Policy: The Labour Party in the 1930s* (1969), 22.
5. See *eg*, M. A. Fitzsimmons, *The Foreign Policy of the British Labour Government, 1945–51* (Indiana, 1953), 23–24; A. F. Havighurst, *Twentieth Century Britain* (New York, 1962), 385; Lord Strang, *Britain in World Affairs* (New York), 338–9.
6. See R. E. Dowse, *Left in the Centre: The Independent Labour Party; 1893–1940* (Evanston, USA, 1966), 152–202.
7. See Ben Pimlott, 'The Socialist League: Intellectuals and the Labour Left in the 1930s', in *Journal of Contemporary History*, vol. 6, no. 3 (1971).
8. H. Pelling, *A Short History of the Labour Party* (1961), 71.
9. *Ibid.*, 79.

CHAPTER I

1. 351 HC Deb., 293.
2. Labour's pro-German reputation in the 1920s was, however, ill-founded. See Naylor, *op. cit.*, 5.

3. Compare *eg*, Naylor, *op. cit.*, 313; H. Pelling, *Britain and the Second World War* (1970), 12.
4. H. Dalton, *Memoirs, 1931–45: The Fateful Years* (1957), 263.
5. 351 HC Deb., 293.
6. H. Morrison, *An Autobiography* (1960), 168.
7. M. Foot, *Aneurin Bevan*, vol. I: *1897–1955* (1962), 304.
8. E. Hyams, *The New Statesman: The History of the First Fifty Years* (1963), 214.
9. 351 HC Deb., 299 (September 3, 1939).
10. LPCR, *1940*, 8.
11. Dalton, *Diaries*, August 30, 1939.
12. LPCR, *1940*, 8.
13. NEC, Minutes, September 2, 1939.
14. Dalton, *The Fateful Years*, 265.
15. 351 HC Deb., 282 (September 2, 1939).
16. L. S. Amery, *My Political Life*, vol. III: *The Unforgiving Years* (1955), 324.
17. Dalton, *Papers*, Subject File, 15–27.
18. 351 HC Deb., 133.
19. *Ibid.*, 116–17.
20. TUC, Ann. Report, *1939*, 337–8.
21. LPCR, *1939*, 117.
22. Naylor, *op. cit.*, 278.
23. 351 HC Deb., 57.
24. Naylor, *op. cit.*, 314.
25. A. J. P. Taylor, *The Touble Makers: dissent over foreign policy, 1792–1939* (1969 edition, Panther), 181.
26. E. Shinwell, *The Labour Story: Being a History of the Labour Party* (1953), 161.
27. LPCR, *1940*, 6.
28. NEC, Minutes, September 2, 1939. (This meeting, however, did agree that the Party should co-operate with the Ministry of Information.)
29. Dalton, *Diaries*, September 6, 1939.
30. C. R. Attlee, *As It Happened* (1954), 105.
31. Dalton, *Diaries*, September 6, 1939.
32. Attlee, *Papers (U.)*, Box 8.
33. *New Statesman*, September 9, 1939. This was also the title of a book by Dalton, *viz.*, H. Dalton, *Hitler's War: Before and After* (Middlesex, 1940).
34. LPCR, *1940*, 7. The statement was entitled 'Why Kill Each Other?'.
35. Dalton, *Diaries*, June 30, 1939.
36. LPCR, *1940*, 8–9.
37. Dalton, *Diaries*, August 25–31, 1939. The *Message* had been proposed to the NCL by Dalton himself.
38. 351 HC Deb., 293.

Notes

39. TUC, Ann. Report, *1939*, 288, 337–8.
40. *Tribune*, September 15, 1939.
41. *New Statesman*, September 9, 1939.

CHAPTER II

1. LPCR, *1940*, 8–9.
2. J. Harvey, ed., *The Diplomatic Diaries of Oliver Harvey, 1937–40* (1970), 322.
3. *New Statesman*, October 14, 1939.
4. *Tribune*, September 8, 1939.
5. Hyams, *op. cit.*, 54.
6. *Tribune*, September 8, 1939.
7. *Ibid.*, September 22, 1939.
8. *Daily Herald*, September 18, 1939.
9. 351 HC Deb., 1862, October 3, 1939.
10. *Ibid.*, 1883.
11. *Tribune*, October 6, 1939.
12. 352 HC Deb., 583–588.
13. *Tribune*, October 13, 1939.
14. Telegram to PM of Canada, October 12, 1939 (CAB 21/952).
15. Dalton, *Diaries*, September 18, October 12, 23, 30, 1939.
16. *See eg*, Amery, *op. cit.*, 333.
17. P. Addison, 'Lloyd George and Compromise Peace in the Second World War', in *Lloyd George: Twelve Essays*, ed. by A. J. P. Taylor (1971), 336–71. I am also indebted to this source for the two quotations which follow.
18. In 1940, Stokes was also in contact with Beaverbrook who, for a time, appeared to favour Stokes's views (A. J. P. Taylor, *Beaverbrook* [1972], 403–4).
19. 351 HC Deb., 1871–2.
20. H. Nicolson, *Diaries*, October 17, 1939.
21. Quoted in Addison, *op. cit.*, 371.
22. NEC, Minutes, September 27, 1939.
23. 351 HC Deb., 1862.
24. 352 HC Deb., 568–70.
25. This document was based on a draft by P. J. Noel-Baker, and subsequently reconsidered by Noel-Baker, Laski and Dalton.
26. NEC, Minutes, October 25, 1939.
27. C. R. Attlee, *Labour's Peace Aims* (December 5, 1939).
28. H. Pelling, *A History of British Trade Unionism* (Middlesex, 1963), 211.
29. This was issued as a pamphlet: H. Morrison, *What Are We Fighting For?* (November 27, 1939).
30. 355 HC Deb., 22–3.

175

31. H. Laski, *The Labour Party, The War and The Future* (November 1939).
32. G. D. H. Cole, *War Aims* (November 1939). According to the *New Statesman*, November 25, 1939, Cole's pamphlet sold out its first edition of 15,000 copies. As well, there was a second edition (also published by the *New Statesman*), and a Left Book Club edition.
33. *Daily Herald*, November 14, 1939. The following were the signatories: J. Barr, G. Buchanan, W. G. Cove, T. E. Groves, Agnes Hardie, David Kirkwood, George Lansbury, W. Leonard, Neil Maclean, M. K. Macmillan, George Mathers, H. G. McGhee, F. Messer, J. Rhys Davies, Alfred Salter, S. Silverman, A. Sloan, W. R. Sorensen, R. R. Stokes, Cecil Wilson.
34. Foot, *op. cit.*, 304.
35. *Tribune*, November 17, 1939.
36. 'Vigilans' could well have been Zilliacus. *See* Taylor, *The Trouble-Makers*, 165.
37. *Ibid.*, November 24.

CHAPTER III

1. 355 HC Deb., 291.
2. LPCR, *1940*, 13.
3. Noel-Baker represented the Party, Citrine the TUC, and J. Downie the Co-operative Union.
4. Dalton, *The Fateful Years*, 293.
5. The delegation included Attlee, George Dallas, Dalton, Noel-Baker, James Walker, Mrs Ayrton-Gould and W. Gillies (NEC, Minutes, March 20, 1940).
6. Dalton, *The Fateful Years*, 290n.
7. *Ibid.*, 292.
8. Calder, *The People's War: Britain, 1939–45* (1969), 75.
9. NEC, Minutes, March 20, 1940. The motion to expel Pritt was carried by 17 votes to 3. James Walker usually took the lead in such matters. Of the minority, Ellen Wilkinson and Susan Lawrence were almost certainly included as they had tried to defer consideration of the matter but had been defeated by the same majority. According to *Tribune* (April 12, 1940), Laski's was the third vote.
10. *Tribune*, February 23, 1940.
11. *New Statesman*, March 23, 1940.
12. *Tribune*, March 22, 1, 15; April 12, 3, 1940.
13. NEC, Minutes, January 25, 1940.
14. Addison, *op. cit.*, 371.
15. Lloyd George, *Papers*, G/19/3. Stokes to Lloyd George, June 1940.
16. The Emergency Executive Committee had, in turn, set up a special sub-

committee to consider the draft; the latter's membership was Mrs B.
Ayrton-Gould, James Walker, George Dallas (who was chairman of the
International Sub-Committee of the NEC), and Dalton (NEC, Minutes,
February 6, 1940).

17. *Ibid.*
18. Dalton, *Diaries*, Middle of February, 1940.
19. *Ibid.*
20. *Ibid.*, September 18, 1939.
21. NEC, Minutes, March 20, 1940.
22. For the full text, *see* LPCR, *1940*, 188–90.
23. 356 HC Deb., 1310.
24. *Ibid.*, 1415–22.
25. *Daily Herald*, April 22, 1940.
26. H. Laski, *Is This An Imperialist War?* (1940).
27. LPCR, *1940*, 124.
28. *Tribune*, May 10, 1940.
29. *Ibid.*, May 3, 1940.
30. M. Foot, *op. cit.*, 315.
31. H. Morrison, *An Autobiography*, 172.
32. Amery, *op. cit.*, 258.
33. Morrison, *op. cit.*, 172–3 (Morrison's claim is disputed in Calder, *op. cit.*, 82).
34. A. J. P. Taylor, *English History, 1914–1945* (1965), 472*n*.
35. The Granada Historical Records Interview, *Clem Attlee* (1967), 22.
36. Pelling, *Britain and the Second World War*, 71. Addison, however, interprets this as a ploy to introduce Lloyd George into the cabinet (Addison, *op. cit.*, 372).
37. NEC, Minutes, May 10, 1940.
38. *Ibid.*, May 11, 1940.
39. LPCR, *1940*, 123.
40. *eg*, HC Deb., 1086–94, 1178.
41. 351 HC Deb., 295 (September 3, 1939).
42. Dalton, *The Fateful Years*, 201–3. Also see, Dalton, *Papers*, 'Personal Papers A–Z, 1941 and 1942', Dalton's Note of a Conversation with Oliver Stanley, April 28, 1941.
43. Hyams, *op. cit.*, 215.
44. LPCR, *1940*, 137.

CHAPTER IV

1. Alan Bullock, *The Life and Times of Ernest Bevin*, vol. II: *Minister of Labour, 1940–45* (1967), 109.
2. A. J. P. Taylor, *Beaverbrook* (1972), 516.

3. Sir Llewellyn Woodward, *British Foreign Policy During the Second World War* (1962), xliii.
4. W. S. Churchill, *The Second World War*, vol. II: *Their Finest Hour* (Cassell, new edition 1950), 9.
5. CAB 65/13, May 26; June 3, 1940.
6. *Tribune*, May 24, 1940.
7. *Ibid.*, May 31, 1940.
8. *Ibid.*, June 7, 1940.
9. Churchill, *Their Finest Hour*, 9.
10. C. R. Attlee, *et al.*, *Churchill by His Contemporaries: An Observer Appreciation* (1965), 59.
11. H. Nicolson, *Diaries and Letters, 1939–45*, ed. by N. Nicolson (1967), 106 (August 11, 1940).
12. A. J. P. Taylor, *English History*, 479.
13. *Tribune*, May 24, 1940.
14. Cripps owed his post principally to Churchill and Halifax. See, Sir Llewellyn Woodward, *British Foreign Policy in the Second World War*, vol. I (1970), 459–61. See also, *Clem Attlee, op. cit.*, 24; and Churchill, *Their Finest Hour*, 118.
15. Dalton, *Papers*, 'Personal Papers A–Z, 1938–40', Box III. Dalton to Halifax, July 2, 1940.
16. David Dilks, ed., *The Diaries of Sir Alexander Cadogan, 1938–1945* (1971), 312.
17. *Ibid.*, 313.
18. Cited by Dilks, *ibid.*
19. Woodward, *op. cit.*, vol. I, 464–501.
20. *Ibid.*, 598.
21. Nicolson, *Diaries and Letters*, 99.
22. CAB 21/1581.
23. CAB 87/9, October 4, 1940.
24. Nicolson, *Diaries and Letters*, 102–3, 139, and 139*n* (by N. Nicolson).
25. CAB 65/17, January 20, 1941.
26. Nicolson, *op. cit.*, 144.
27. See, *eg, The Times*, July 18, 1940; *Daily Express*, May 31, 1940.
28. *Tribune*, May 31, 1940.
29. K. Martin, *Harold Laski: (1893–1950): A Biographical Memoir* (1953), 126, 139, 140–1.
30. H. Laski, *Where Do We Go From Here?* (Middlesex, 1940).
31. H. Laski, *et al.*, *Programme For Victory* (January 1941).
32. Dalton, *Diaries*, November 5, 1940.
33. NEC, Minutes, November 5, 1940.
34. Martin, *Laski*, 158.

35. PREM 4, 62/5. Laski to Churchill, February 10, 1941. Churchill was content to thank Laski and assure him that his letter would be studied.
36. This consisted of twelve members. In the October 1942 elections, Bevan and Stokes received less than 40 votes each, and were not elected. Shinwell scraped into eleventh place. Those at the top of the list secured just over 100 votes. 'Here was a gauge of the general temper of the Labour Party ...' Foot comments (*ibid.*, 394).
37. James Griffiths, *Pages From Memory* (1969), 69.
38. He was not impressed with the importance of the office which was offered to him, and rejected it without consulting Attlee (Dalton, *Diaries*, May 18, 1940; 'Note of a Conversation with Attlee'). This did not prevent Attlee from trying to find another post for Shinwell 'to keep him quiet' (*ibid.*, June 8, 1940).
39. Cited in Addison, *op. cit.*, 376.
40. *Tribune*, November 1, 1940.
41. *Ibid.*, December 20, 1940.
42. These broadcasts were subsequently published; Lord Vansittart, *Black Record: Germans Past and Present* (1941). There were thirteen reprints in 1941 alone.
43. *Daily Herald*, December 10, 1940.
44. *Tribune*, March 21, 1941.
45. Dalton, *Hitler's War*, 136, 141, 145.
46. *Clem Attlee*, 53.
47. Dalton, *Diaries*, July 26, 1940.
48. *Ibid.*, January 30, 1941.
49. *Ibid.*, January 5, 1941.
50. NEC, Minutes, April 23, 1941.
51. LPCR, *1941*, 3, 4, 5, 132, 133, 134, 138, 158 (The 'War' section was adopted by 2,430,000 votes to 19,000; 'Peace' by 2,413,000 to 30,000).
52. Dalton, *Diaries*, June 3, 1941.

CHAPTER V

1. *New Statesman*, March 22, 1941.
2. *Ibid.*, August 23, 1941.
3. *Daily Herald*, November 17, 1941.
4. NEC, Minutes, File no. 85.
5. *Middleton Papers*, Box 9.
6. *Ibid.*, Box 11. (Almost all were released fairly soon afterwards.)
7. NEC, Minutes, File no. 85.
8. Dalton, *Diaries*, November 21, 1941.

9. NEC, Minutes, Box 85.
10. In February 1942, 'Fight For Freedom' sponsored the publication of Curt Geyer's *Hitler's New Order – Kaiser's Old Order* whose object, in the author's own blunt words, was 'to prove that the political ambitions of Germany under Hitler and under the Kaiser [were] identical in the sphere of foreign policy' (Preface).

Victor Gollancz, the Left-wing publisher, replied to Vansittart's *Black Record* in a book entitled *Shall Our Children Live or Die?* 'Fight For Freedom' riposted in April 1942 with *Gollancz in German Wonderland* by Geyer and Walter Loeb. The latter contained a Foreword by James Walker, MP, who described it as 'a complete and crushing reply to the wishful thinking and vague theorizing about Germany that is contained in Gollancz's book . . . German mentality,' Walker asserted, was 'quite different from the mentality of other nations in Europe'. This was an odd remark considering that Geyer and Loeb were both Germans!

In September 1942, Gollancz produced an émigré writer of his own, Julius Braunthal, who maintained in *Need Germany Survive?* that for a Socialist the German problem was of interest merely as an aspect of the European problem. Harold Laski wrote an introduction to Braunthal's book, inveighing against 'the nonsense which seeks to make the German national character the vital factor in the emergence of Hitlerism'.
11. *New Statesman*, April 18, 1942.
12. *Labour Party Archives*, Gillies to Dallas, February 13, 1942.
13. Dalton, *Diaries*, February 16, 1942.
14. International Sub-Committee of the NEC, Minutes, March 24, 1942.
15. NEC, Minutes, April 22, 1942.
16. May be seen in NEC, Minutes, file 86.
17. NEC, Minutes, April 22, 1942.
18. The Labour Party, *The Old World and the New Society* (1942).
19. LPCR, *1942*, 9.
20. *Ibid.*, 153.
21. Dalton, *Diaries*, May 22, 1942.
22. *New Statesman*, May 23, and June 6, 1942.
23. TUC, Ann. Report, *1942*, 11.
24. LPCR, *1943*, 38.
25. *Tribune*, September 4, 1942.
26. *New Statesman*, October 17, 1942.
27. *Ibid.*
28. *Tribune*, September 11, 1942.
29. *Ibid.*
30. *Ibid.*
31. *Middleton Papers*, Box 6, 'Fight For Freedom' file.

32. Dalton, *Papers*, 'Personal Papers A–Z, 1941 and 1942' (the memorandum is dated August 28, 1942).
33. CAB 66/31, 532, November 19, 1942.
34. Dalton, *op. cit.*, Dalton to Eden, November 19, 1942.
35. Dalton, *Diaries*, November 17, 1942.
36. The Inter-departmental Committee on Reparations and Economic Security.
37. Dalton, *Diaries*, November 10, 18, 24, 25, 1942.
38. G. Dallas, H. Clay, J. Walker, T. Williamson, W. Gillies, J. Middleton.
39. LPCR, *1943*, 39.
40. *Labour Party Archives.*

CHAPTER VI

1. *Tribune*, July 4, 1941.
2. 374 HC Deb., 1977 (October 27, 1941).
3. 376 HC Deb., 119–21, 140–4 (November 13, 1941).
4. The vote of confidence on the Greek campaign was taken on May 7, 1941, and carried by 476 votes to 3. Shinwell himself was among the abstainers, but Bevan voted with the government.
5. M. Howard, *The Mediterranean Strategy in the Second World War* (1968), 13.
6. Taylor, *Beaverbrook*, 475–6.
7. CAB 66/22, 311, July 21, 1942.
8. A. Bryant, *The Turn of the Tide; the Alanbrooke Diaries* (1957), 340.
9. Dilks, ed., *The Cadogan Diaries*, 440.
10. Taylor, *Beaverbrook*, 522–47.
11. Taylor, *English History*, 536.
12. CAB 65/30, 54th conclusions, April 29, 1942.
13. CAB 69/4, Defence Committee (Operations) 1940–45, April 14, 1942.
14. CAB 65/30, 73rd conclusions, June 11, 1942.
15. *Tribune*, November 13, 1942.
16. 377 HC Deb., 592, 624, 788–90, January 27, 1942.
17. Calder, *op. cit.*, 272.
18. Taylor, *English History*, 542–3.
19. Taylor, *Beaverbrook*, 508–16.
20. K. Young, *Churchill and Beaverbrook: A Study in Friendship and Politics* (1966), 228.
21. 380 HC Deb., 332, 333, May 19, 1942.
22. See Foot's comment, *op. cit.*, 377.
23. 381 HC Deb., 271, 272, 283, 529, 540, July 1, 1942.
24. Taylor, *English History*, 554.
25. Dalton, *Diaries*, December 8, 1942.

26. LPCR, *1942*, 52–3. Attlee had previously told a PLP meeting that if a substantial number voted against the government he would find his own position impossible (Nicolson, *Diaries and Letters*, 192).

27. The eight were: Aneurin Bevan, Fred Bellenger, F. G. Bowles, Dr L. Haden-Guest, B. V. Kirby, Sydney Silverman, R. R. Stokes and Neil Maclean.

28. Nicolson, *op. cit.*, 237.

29. For an account of the CommonWealth Party, see D. L. Prynn, 'CommonWealth – a British "Third Party" of the 1940s', in *Journal of Contemporary History*, vol. 7, nos. 1 and 2, January–April 1972, 169–79.

30. *Tribune*, April 3, 1942.

31. *Tribune*, November 27, 1942.

32. 385 HC Deb., 461 (November 18, 1942).

33. *Tribune*, December 11, 1942.

34. Cited in Bullock, *op. cit.*, 202–3.

35. LPCR, *1942*, 56.

36. Martin, *Laski*, 126, 127, 144.

37. NEC, Minutes, March 26, 1942.

38. *Ibid.*, April 9, 1942.

39. LPCR, *1942*, 94–112.

40. *New Statesman*, June 6, 1942.

41. NEC, Minutes, October 28 and November 25, 1942.

42. 385 HC Deb., 133 (November 12, 1942).

43. *Tribune*, February 12, 1943.

44. *Ibid.*, January 1, 1943.

45. Nicolson, *Diaries and Letters*, 277.

46. *Tribune*, March 5, 1943. Though Bevan, it should be noted, believed at this time that a second front proper would be started in 1943.

47. Martin, *Laski*, 136.

48. CAB 65/40, 140 conclusions, October 14, 1943.

CHAPTER VII

1. LPCR, *1941*.

2. Attlee, *Papers (U.)*, Box 8.

3. PREM 4, 21/3. Note from Eden to Churchill, August 22, 1941.

4. Sir Llewellyn Woodward, *British Foreign Policy in the Second World War*, vol. II (1971), 7, 8.

5. G. D. H. Cole, *Europe, Russia and the Future* (September 1941), 13, 16.

6. Woodward, *op. cit.*, vol. II, 11–12, 24, 31–2, 43.

7. *Ibid.*, 46, 51.

8. I. Maisky, *Memoirs of a Soviet Ambassador: The War 1939–43* (1967), 232.

9. CAB 65/24, 131 conclusions, minute 2, December 19, 1941.
10. Woodward, *op. cit.*, 200.
11. Churchill, *The Second World War*, vol. III: *The Grand Alliance* (1950), 393.
12. Woodward, *op. cit.*, 200–1.
13. CAB 66/20, 282, November 24, 1941.
14. Woodward, *op. cit.*, 237.
15. Dilks, ed., *op. cit.*, 439. Note by Dilks.
16. CAB 66/22.
17. CAB 65/29, 17 conclusions, minute 5, February 6, 1942.
18. Cited in Young, *op. cit.*, 235.
19. Taylor, *Beaverbrook*, 515.
20. Dalton, *Diaries*, January 28, 1941.
21. Taylor, *op. cit.*, 507–8.
22. CAB 66/22.
23. Dalton, *Papers*, 'Personal Papers A–Z, 1941–42'.
24. CAB, *op. cit.*
25. CAB 65/29, 25 conclusions, February 25, 1942.
26. Churchill, *The Second World War*, vol. IV: *The Hinge of Fate* (1951), 293
27. CAB, *op. cit.*, 24 conclusions.
28. *Ibid.*, 37 conclusions, March 25, 1942.
29. Woodward, *op. cit.*, 241.
30. Dilks, ed., *op. cit.*, 455.
31. CAB 65/30, 66 conclusions, May 25, 1942.
32. CAB 66/24, 219 (revised), May 22, 1942.
33. CAB 65/30, May 25, 1942.
34. CAB 65/30, 68 conclusions, minute 2, May 26, 1942. See also Dilks, ed., *op. cit.*, 455.
35. CAB, *op. cit.* (Molotov's usually reluctant political elbow might have been jostled by the fact that the three Russian spring offensives had all ended in disaster.)
36. Woodward, *British Foreign Policy During the Second World War* (1962), 433.
37. *Ibid.*, 434.
38. CAB 66/31, 532, November 19, 1942.
39. Bullock, *op. cit.*, 205.
40. CAB 65/32, 164 conclusions, minute 1, December 3, 1942.
41. CAB 65/37, 12 conclusions, minute 9, January 20, 1943.

CHAPTER VIII

1. Dalton, *Diaries*, January 5, 1943.
2. PREM 4, 21/5, May 23, 1943.
3. PREM 4, 30/3, June 1943.

4. Woodward, *op. cit.*, 438, 441–2, 439.
5. CAB 65/38, 53 conclusions, minute 2, April 13, 1943.
6. Woodward, *op. cit.*, 442.
7. CAB 65/38, 75 conclusions, minute 1, May 23, 1943.
8. CAB 66/37, 217.
9. *Ibid.*, 243, June 15, 1943.
10. CAB 65/34, 86 conclusions, June 16, 1943.
11. CAB 87/65, 322.
12. CAB 66/39, 321.
13. CAB 78/11, July 21, 1943.
14. CAB 65/39, 119 conclusions, minute 1, August 25, 1943.
15. *Ibid.*, 120 conclusions, minute 4, August 30, 1943.
16. CAB 65/40, 147 conclusions, minute 1, October 27, 1943.
17. *Ibid.*, 150 conclusions, minute 1, November 4, 1943.
18. CAB 87/65, PS (43), 2.
19. A. Eden, *The Eden Memoirs: The Reckoning* (1965), 425.
20. Lord Strang, *At Home and Abroad* (1956), 200. (My emphasis.)
21. W. S. Churchill, *The Second World War*, vol. VI: *Triumph and Tragedy* (1954), 244.
22. HC Deb., 1654–6, December 15, 1943.
23. PREM 4, 30/5, Note to Eden, November 1, 1943.
24. Woodward, *op. cit.*, 446–7.
25. Strang, *op. cit.*, 202.
26. CAB 87/83, ACA (43), November 26, 1943; CAB 66/43, WP (43), 519; CAB 65/38, WM (43), 155 conclusions, minute 5, November 16, 1943.
27. CAB 87/83, COS (43), 311, December 12, 1943.
28. *Ibid.*

CHAPTER IX

1. LPCR, *1943*, 3.
2. 391 HC Deb., 2202–3.
3. 386 HC Deb., 1512.
4. *New Statesman*, February 6, 1943.
5. *Tribune*, May 21, 1943.
6. *New Statesman*, May 29, 1943.
7. *Tribune*, May 14, 1943.
8. W. Derkow, *The Other Germany: Facts and Figures* (May 1943).
9. Dalton, *Diaries*, June 13, 1943; NEC, Minutes, June 13, 1943.
10. LPCR, *1943*, 116–17, 176–8, 184–6.
11. See, *eg*, *Tribune*, July 2, September 24, 1943; Foot, *op. cit.*, 423; *New Statesman*, June 24, July 3, 1943.

12. NEC (International sub-committee), Minutes, September 14, 1943.
13. TUC, Ann. Report, *1943*, 331.
14. Attlee, *Papers (U.)*, Box 8, Noel-Baker to Attlee, September 13, 1943.
15. NEC (International sub-committee), Minutes, September 14, 1943.
16. Attlee, *op. cit.*, September 15.
17. NEC (International sub-committee), Minutes, September 15, 1943.
18. Dalton, *Papers*, Subject Files, 15–27.
19. *Ibid.*, '1944 Miscellaneous', Dalton to Brailsford, March 13, 1944. (Dalton's emphasis.)
20. *New Statesman*, May 29, 1943.
21. *Tribune*, June 18, 1943.
22. *New Statesman*, August 28, 1943.
23. *Ibid.*, July 10, 1943.
24. NEC, Minutes, August 25 and September 22, 1943 (Laski resumed his attendances at the NEC's meetings on October 27, 1943).
25. There was also a considerable feeling of restlessness in another section of the Party at this period concerning the failure of the government to repeal the Trade Union Act of 1927 (*see*, NEC, Minutes, June 1943). The Left did not exploit this issue.
26. 391 HC Deb., 1792, 1929, 2203–13.
27. *Tribune*, June 25, 1943.
28. *Tribune*, May 21, July 2, 9, 1943.
29. 392 HC Deb., 88, 95–6, 101 (September 21, 1943).
30. *New Statesman*, November 6, 1943.
31. 393 HC Deb., 1323–4 (November 11, 1943).
32. *Tribune*, October 15, 22, 1943.
33. *New Statesman*, December 18, 1943.
34. *Ibid.*, December 25, 1943.

CHAPTER X

1. Dalton, *Diaries*, September 16, 1943; July 19, 1944.
2. Dalton, *Papers*, Subject Files, 15–27.
3. NEC (International sub-committee), Minutes, January 11, 1944.
4. LPCR, *1944*.
5. *Tribune*, January 21, 1944.
6. *New Statesman*, January 1, 8, 15, 22, 1944.
7. *Socialist Commentary*, January 1944.
8. Dalton, *Diaries*, January 18, 1944.
9. *Tribune*, February 25, 1944.
10. 397 HC Deb., 901 (February 23, 1944).
11. *Tribune*, March 24, 1944.

12. *Ibid.*, April 7, 14, 1944.
13. Dalton, *Diaries*, April 5, 1944.
14. NEC, Minutes, April 5, 1944.
15. NEC (International sub-committee), Minutes, April 18, 1944.
16. Dalton, *Diaries*, April 18, 1944.
17. *Tribune*, April 28, 1944.
18. *New Statesman*, April 29, May 6, 1944.
19. L. Woolf, *The International Post-War Settlement* (September 1944).
20. Dalton, *Diaries*, October 27, 1944.
21. NEC, Minutes, November 22, 1944.
22. Dalton, *Diaries,* November 22, 1944.
23. TUC, Ann. Report, *1944*, 11–13, 266–8.
24. 400 HC Deb., 815–17 (May 24, 1944).
25. *Ibid.*, 781.
26. 402 HC Deb., 1479.
27. *Tribune*, May 5, 1944. The PLP vote was 60 for expulsion, 71 against.
28. NEC (and Administrative Committee of the PLP), Minutes, May 16, 1944.
29. *Ibid.*, July 26, 1944.
30. 402 HC Deb., 1550–60.
31. See *eg*, 403 HC Deb., 629–35 (September 29, 1944).
32. LPCR, *1944*, 131, 132, 139.
33. Dalton, *Diaries*, December 12, 1944.
34. *Ibid.*, December 13, 1944.

CHAPTER XI

1. Dilks, ed., *op. cit.*, 697.
2. See *eg*, Lord Chandos, *The Memoirs* (1962), 293. (Lord Chandos was Oliver Lyttelton on the APW Committee.)
3. F. Williams, *Nothing So Strange: An Autobiography* (1970), 219.
4. CAB 87/84, Armistice Terms and Civil Administration Committee, January 12, 1944.
5. *Ibid.*, April 3, 1944.
6. CAB 87/67, 1, April 19, 1944.
7. CAB 87/66, June 1, 8, 1944.
8. CAB 66/51, 345, June 26, 1944.
9. CAB 87/67, 43, July 11, 1944.
10. *Ibid.*, 47, July 19, 1944.
11. CAB 87/66, July 20, 1944.
12. CAB 87/67, 52.
13. CAB 87/66, July 27, 1944.
14. *Ibid.*, August 31, 1944.

15. Woodward, *op. cit.*, 471.
16. CAB 87/68, 88. Foreign Office to Foreign Secretary at Quebec, September 14, 1944.
17. Woodward, *op. cit.*, 472.
18. CAB 87/66.
19. Woodward, *op. cit.*, 474.
20. D. C. Watt, *Britain Looks to Germany* (1965), 41.
21. J. F. Snell, *The War-time Origins of the East-West Dilemma Over Germany* (New Orleans, 1959), 85.
22. This came in November 1944 (Cablegram from Roosevelt to Churchill, November 19, 1944. Quoted in *The Times*, June 13, 1972, by Henry Raymont in an article, 'Inside View of Churchill and Roosevelt at War').
23. CAB 87/66, September 21, 1944. See also, Woodward, *op. cit.*, 473, 473*n*, and Churchill, *Triumph and Tragedy*, 141–2.
24. CAB 80/97, COS (44), 'O' Memoranda, September 9, 1944.
25. CAB 79/81, COS 330, October 6, 1944.
26. Woodward, *op. cit.*, 469–70.
27. CAB 87/66, September 21, 1944.
28. CAB 87/68, 105, October 20, 1944.
29. CAB 87/66, November 23, 1944.
30. CAB 87/69, January 3, 1945.
31. *Ibid.*, January 4, 1945.
32. *Ibid.*, February 1, 1945.

CHAPTER XII

1. CAB 87/84, April 20, 1944.
2. CAB 87/66, July 20, 1944.
3. When, in August 1944, the full war cabinet agreed to send troops into Greece in the event of a German withdrawal, Attlee merely commented that it might be politically wise to arrange that the troops be sent ostensibly for the purpose of relief (CAB 65/47, 103 conclusions, Minute 1, August 9, 1944).
4. CAB 87/67, 61, August 19, 1944.
5. CAB 87/66, August 23, 1944.
6. *Ibid.*, August 31, 1944.
7. PREM 21/5, April 29, 1944.
8. CAB 66/53, 463, August 9, 1944.
9. CAB 21/1614 (2).
10. See *eg*, Eden, *The Reckoning*, 354, 386, 453, 456; C. de Gaulle, *War Memoirs: Unity, 1942–44* (1959), 227, 232; Piers Dixon, *Double Diplomat: The Life of Sir Pierson Dixon, Don and Diplomat* (1968), 92–3.

11. CAB 87/66, April 27, 1944.
12. PREM 4, 30/7 (APW, WP (44), 106, July 24, 1944).
13. CAB 65/48, 157 conclusions, November 27, 1944.
14. CAB 21/1614, Prime Minister's personal minute, serial no. M. 1144/4.
15. CAB 66/53, 414, July 26, 1944.
16. CAB 65/47, 111 conclusions, August 28, 1944.
17. The General Sikorski Historical Institute, ed., *Documents on Polish-Soviet Relations 1939–45*, vol. II: *1943–45* (1967), 387–9.
18. CAB 65/48, 157 conclusions, November 27, 1944.
19. *Ibid.*, 143 conclusions, November 1, 1944.
20. CAB 65/51, 7 conclusions, minute 4, January 22, 1945.
21. *Ibid.*, 9 conclusions, minute 4, January 25, 1945.
22. *Ibid.*, 10 conclusions, January 26, 1945.

CHAPTER XIII

1. PREM 4, 81/4, January 15, 1945.
2. 407 HC Deb., 397–8, January 18, 1945.
3. CAB 65/51, 16 conclusions, February 8, 1945.
4. PREM 4, 78/1, Fleece 324 (Part 2), February 9, 1945.
5. CAB 65/51, 18 conclusions, minute 3, February 12, 1945.
6. Dalton, *Diaries*, January 16, 1945. (Also present were Shinwell, Laski, Noel-Baker, Jennie Adamson, Tom Williamson and Dalton.)
7. Bullock, *op. cit.*, 348–9.
8. Quoted in *The Times*, February 28, 1945.
9. *Daily Herald*, February 10, 1945.
10. C. Cooke, *The Life of Richard Stafford Cripps* (1957), 321–2.
11. CAB 65/49, 2 conclusions, January 8, 1945.
12. 408 HC Deb., 1616–19.
13. PREM 4, 78/1, Fleece 449, February 15, 1945.
14. 408 HC Deb., 1267, 1421–2, 1267 (February 27, 1945).
15. *eg, Tribune*, May 4, 1945.
16. *New Statesman*, January 27, 1945.
17. *Tribune*, January 12, 1945.
18. CAB 66/63, 146, March 7, 1945.
19. Woodward, *op. cit.*, 524.
20. CAB 65/51, 35 conclusions, minute 3, March 22, 1945.
21. CAB 65/52, 48 conclusions, minute 7, April 20, 1945.
22. Bevan, however, objected (see NEC, Minutes, May 9, 18, 20, 21, 1945).
23. CAB 87/69, April 13, 1945.
24. *Ibid.*, 57, April 19; 59, April 23; 60, April 25, 1945.
25. CAB 65/52, 39 conclusions, minute 1, April 3, 1945.

26. CAB 65/50, 43 conclusions, April 12, 1945.
27. *New Statesman*, March 24, April 21, 1945.
28. *Tribune*, February 23, 1945.
29. Dalton, *Diaries*, March 3, 4, 1945.
30. Labour Party Advisory Committee on International Questions, 'The Future of Anglo-French Relations' (unpublished document, Labour Party Archives. Dated December 1944; revised March 1945).
31. LPCR, *1945*, 119.
32. HC Deb., 1621.
33. Bullock, *op. cit.*, 349.
34. *Tribune*, March 2, 1945.
35. Dalton, *Diaries*, May 16, 1945.
36. *Ibid.*
37. LPCR, *1945*, 104.
38. *Ibid.*, 107.
39. *Ibid.*, 107, 78-9, 110-14, 118.

CHAPTER XIV

1. *New Statesman*, May 12, 19.
2. Dixon, *op. cit.*, 155.

Selected Bibliography*

A. PERSONAL MANUSCRIPTS

C. R. Attlee, Papers. University College, Oxford.
E. Bevin, Papers. Churchill College, Cambridge.
H. Dalton, Diaries and Papers. London School of Economics, London.
D. Lloyd George, Papers. Beaverbrook Library, London.
J. Middleton, Papers. Labour Party Archives, Transport House, London.
H. Nicolson, Diaries. Balliol College, Oxford.

B. GOVERNMENT DOCUMENTS AND DEBATES, 1939–45

British Government. Cabinet Papers.
——. Chiefs of Staff Papers.
——. Prime Minister's Office Papers.
General Sikorski Historical Institute. *Documents on Polish-Soviet Relations, 1939–45.* Vol. II: *1943–45* (1967).
Great Britain. *House of Commons, Official Report.* Fifth Series, vols. 351–410.

C. LABOUR PARTY† AND TRADES UNION CONGRESS PAPERS AND REPORTS

Labour Party. *Reports of the Annual Conference, 1939–45.*
——. Advisory Committee on International Questions. 'The Future of Anglo-French Relations.' (December 1944. Revised, March 1945.)
——. Advisory Committee on International Questions. 'The Re-Education of Germany and the Satellite Countries.' (1945.)
——. International sub-committee of the National Executive Committee. 'Armistice.' (1943.)
——. International sub-committee of the National Executive Committee. Minutes, 1939–45.
——. Miscellaneous Papers.
——. National Executive Committee. Minutes, 1939–45.
Trades Union Congress. *Report of the Proceedings of the Annual Conference, 1939–45.*

* Place of publication of published works, unless otherwise stated, is London.
† At Transport House, London.

Selected Bibliography

D. PAMPHLETS

1. Labour Party Official Publications

Attlee, C. R. *Labour's Peace Aims: Labour Party Pamphlet No. 5* (December 1939).

Labour Party. *Labour Looks Ahead* (March 1942).

——. *The Old World and The New Society* (1942).

——. National Executive Committee. *The International Post-War Settlement* (April 1944).

Laski, H. *Is This an Imperialist War?* (1940).

——. *The Labour Party, The War, and The Future* (November 1939).

Morrison, H. *What Are We Fighting For?* (November 1939).

2. Others

Cole, G. D. H. *War Aims* (November 1939).

Derkow, W. *The Other Germany: Facts and Figures* (May 1943).

Parliamentary Peace Aims Groups. *Labour and the Post-War International Settlement* (July 1944).

Woolf, L. *The International Post-War Settlement* (September 1944).

E. AUTOBIOGRAPHIES, BIOGRAPHIES AND MEMOIRS

Amery, L. S. *My Political Life*. Vol. III: *The Unforgiving Years* (1955).

Attlee, C. R. *As It Happened* (1954).

Birkenhead, Earl of. *Halifax: The Life of Lord Halifax* (1965).

Brome, V. *Aneurin Bevan* (1953).

Bryant, A. *The Alanbrooke War Diaries: The Turn of the Tide* (1957).

——. *The Alanbrooke War Diaries: Triumph in the West* (1959).

Bullock, A. *The Life and Times of Ernest Bevin*. Vol. II: *Minister of Labour, 1940–45* (1967).

Chandos, Lord. *The Memoirs* (1962).

Churchill, W. S. *The Second World War*. Vol. II: *Their Finest Hour* (new edition, 1950).

——. *The Second World War*. Vol. III: *The Grand Alliance* (1950).

——. *The Second World War*. Vol. IV: *The Hinge of Fate* (1951).

——. *The Second World War*. Vol. VI: *Triumph and Tragedy* (1954).

Citrine, Lord. *Two Careers: A second volume of autobiography* (1967).

Cooke, C. *The Life of Richard Stafford Cripps* (1957).

Dalton, H. *Memoirs, 1931–45: The Fateful Years* (1957).

Dilks, D., ed. *The Diaries of Sir Alexander Cadogan. 1938–45* (1971).

Dixon, P. *Double Diplomat: The Life of Sir Pierson Dixon, Don and Diplomat* (1968).

Eden, A. *The Eden Memoirs: The Reckoning* (1965).

Foot, M. *Aneurin Bevan: A Biography*. Vol. I: *1897–1945* (1962).

de Gaulle, C. *War Memoirs: Unity, 1942–44* (1959).

Granada Historical Records Interview. *Clem Attlee* (1967).

Griffiths, J. *Pages from Memory* (1969).

Harvey, J., ed. *The Diplomatic Diaries of Oliver Harvey, 1937–40* (1970).

Ismay, Lord, *The Memoirs* (1960).

Maisky, I. *Memoirs of a Soviet Ambassador: The War 1939–43* (1967).

Martin, K. *Harold Laski (1893–1950): A biographical memoir* (1953).

Montgomery, Lord. *Memoirs* (1958).

Morrison, H. *Herbert Morrison: An Autobiography* (1960).

Nicolson, H. *Diaries and Letters, 1939–45*. Ed. N. Nicolson (1967).

Strang, Lord. *At Home and Abroad* (1956).

Taylor, A. J. P. *Beaverbrook* (1972).

Williams, F. *Nothing So Strange: An Autobiography* (1970).

F. GENERAL AND DESCRIPTIVE WORKS

Attlee, C. R. *War Comes to Britain* (1940).

——, et al. *Churchill by His Contemporaries: An Observer Appreciation* (1965).

——, et al. *Labour's Aims in War and Peace* (1940).

Brailsford, H. N. *Our Settlement With Germany* (Middlesex, 1944).

Brand, C. F. *The British Labour Party: A Short History* (Stanford, California, USA, 1964).

Braunthal, J. *Need Germany Survive?* (September 1942).

Butler, J. R. M. *Grand Strategy*. Vol. II: *September 1939–June 1941* (1957).

Calder, A. *The People's War: Britain, 1939–45* (1969).

Cole, G. D. H. *A History of the Labour Party from 1914* (1948).

——. *Europe, Russia and the Future* (September 1941).

Dalton, H. *Hitler's War: Before and After* (Middlesex, March 1940).

Dowse, R. E. *Left in the Centre: The Independent Labour Party; 1893–1940* (London, 1966 and Evanston, USA, 1966).

Fitzsimmons, M. A. *The Foreign Policy of the British Labour Government, 1945–51* (Indiana, USA, 1953).

Franklin, W. 'Zonal Boundaries and Access to Berlin', in *World Politics*, No. 1 (October 1963).

Geyer, C. *Hitler's New Order—Kaiser's Old Order* (February 1942).

——, and W. Loeb. *Gollancz in German Wonderland* (April 1942).

Gollancz, V. *Shall Our Children Live Or Die?* (1942).

Gordon, M. R. *Conflict and Consensus in Labour's Foreign Policy, 1914–65* (California, USA, 1969).

Hancock, W. K., and M. M. Gowing. *British War Economy* (1949).

Havighurst, A. F. *Twentieth-Century Britain* (New York, USA, 1962).

Howard, M. *The Mediterranean Strategy in the Second World War* (1968).

Hyams, E. *The New Statesman: The History of the First Fifty Years* (1963).

Laski, H. *Where Do We Go From Here?* (Middlesex, 1940).

———, *et al. Programme For Victory* (January 1941).

Liddell Hart, B. H. *History of the Second World War* (1970).

Lyman, R. W. *The First Labour Government, 1924* (1957).

Maddox, W. P. *Foreign Relations in British Labour Politics* (Cambridge, Mass., USA, 1934).

Malament, B. 'Review of *Socialism and Foreign Policy: Theory and Practice in Britain to 1931*, by K. E. Millar', in *Journal of Modern History*, vol. 42, no. 2 (June 1970).

Martin, K. *Propaganda's Harvest* (October 1941).

Meehan, E. J. *The British Left-Wing and Foreign Policy* (New Brunswick, Canada, 1960).

Miliband, R. *Parliamentary Socialism: A Study in the Politics of Labour* (1961).

Mosely, P. E. *The Kremlin and World Affairs* (New York, USA, 1960).

Naylor, J. F. *Labour's International Policy; the Labour Party in the 1930s* (1969).

Orwell, G. *The Collected Essays, Journalism and Letters*. Vol. II: *My Country Right or Left*. Edited by Sonia Orwell and Ian Angus (Middlesex, 1970).

Pelling, H. *Britain and the Second World War* (1970).

———. *A History of British Trade Unionism* (Middlesex, 1963).

———. *A Short History of the Labour Party* (1961).

Pimlott, Ben. 'The Socialist League: Intellectuals and the Labour Left in the 1930s', in *Journal of Contemporary History*, vol. 6, no. 3, 1971.

Prynn, D. L. 'CommonWealth – a British "Third Party" of the 1940s', in *Journal of Contemporary History*, vol. 7, nos. 1 and 2 (January–April 1972).

Rose, C. R. 'The Relation of Socialist Principles to British Labour's Foreign Policy, 1945–51.' Unpublished Ph.D. thesis, Nuffield College, Oxford, 1959.

Seyd, P. 'Review of *The Gaitskellites*, by S. Haseler', in *Society For the Study of Labour History: Bulletin 21* (Autumn 1970).

Shinwell, E. *The Labour Story: Being a History of the Labour Party* (1953).

Snell, J. F. *The War-time Origins of the East-West Dilemma Over Germany* (New Orleans, USA, 1959).

Stansky, P., ed. *The Left and the War: The British Labour Party and World War I* (New York, USA, 1969).

Strang, Lord. *Britain in World Affairs* (New York, USA, 1961).

Taylor, A. J. P. *English History: 1914–1945* (Oxford University Press, 1965).

———. *The Trouble-Makers: dissent over foreign policy, 1792–1939* (1969 edition).

———, ed. *Lloyd George: Twelve Essays* (1971).

———, *et al. Churchill Revised: A Critical Assessment* (New York, USA, 1968).

Vansittart, Lord. *Black Record: Germans Past and Present* (1941).

Vuckovic, M. N. 'Parliamentary Opinion and British Foreign Policy 1936–38,

with Special Reference to Germany.' Unpublished Ph.D. thesis, McGill
University, 1966.

Watt, D. C. *Britain Looks to Germany* (1965).

Windrich, E. *British Labour's Foreign Policy* (California, USA, 1952).

Winkler, H. R. 'The Emergence of a Labour Foreign Policy in Great Britain,
1918–29', in *Journal of Modern History*, vol. 28, no. 3 (September 1956).

Woodward, Sir E. L. *British Foreign Policy During the Second World War* (1962).

——. *British Foreign Policy in the Second World War*. Vol. I (1970).

——. *British Foreign Policy in the Second World War*. Vol. II (1971).

Young, K. *Churchill and Beaverbrook: A Study in Friendship and Politics* (1966).

G. PERIODICALS AND PRESS, 1939–45

Daily Express
Daily Herald
Manchester Guardian
New Statesman
Socialist Commentary
The Times
Tribune

Index

Index

Acland, Sir Richard, CommonWealth Party, 74; on Greece, 150

Albania, independence, 140

Albu, Austin, and Socialist Clarity group, 63

Alexander, A. V., on conduct of war, 70; German industry, 137, 157

Allied High Commission, Canadian representation at, 126

Amery, L. S., Chamberlain's downfall, 45

Anderson, Sir John, War Cabinet, 48, 91; Bretton Woods Conference, 147-8

Anglo-American Conference (1944), 132, 133, 134

Anglo-Polish Agreement (1939), 19

Anglo-Polish Mutual Assistance Treaty (1939), 19

Anglo-Soviet Agreement (1941), 81, 142

Arcadia Conference, 71

Armistice and Post-War Committee, 125, 138; terms of reference, 126-7; economic policy in Germany, 132, 133; dispute with chiefs of staff, 135; German industry, 137, 157, 158; Hungary, 140; world security system, 142, 143; dismemberment of Germany, 130-1, 151; compulsory military service, 156

Armistice Terms, ad hoc Committee on, 96

Armistice Terms and Civil Administration, Ministerial Committee on, 98, 100, 102, 140; superseded, 125-126

Atlantic Charter, 53, 59, 82-3, 85, 115; and unconditional surrender policy, 104; Dalton's draft on international policy, 117; and occupied Germany, 129; and Yalta, 155

Attlee, Clement, joins Government, 15; outbreak of war, 22; on Russia, 28, 80, 84, 161, 162; anti-Hitler stand, 32; war aims, 33-4, 42, 44, 48, 52; British Communist Party, 38; in coalition, 44-5, 53; Chamberlain's downfall, 45-6; War Cabinet, 48, 49, 50, 51, 90, 91; War Aims Committee, 52; on Dalton, 57; post-war reconstruction, 66, 89, 93, 94-6; conduct of war, 70, 71, 72-4; Party unity, 76, 107; domestic reconstruction, 78; Atlantic Charter, 82-3; Imperial commitment, 95-6, 97; and Italy, 98, 141; Armistice Terms Committee, 98, 100, 126; Labour's International Post-War Settlement, 123; and Bevin, 124; personality and influence, 125, 168; Treatment of Major War Criminals, 127; transfer of German populations, 128; hard line on Germany, 128-30, 138; dismemberment of Germany, 131, 136, 157, 168; Morgenthau plan, 132, 133, 134; German industry, 137; British interests in S.E. Europe, 139-40; and France, 142; Foreign Policy and the Flying Bomb, 143-4; and Poland, 144-5; and Yalta, 151-2, 153, 155; German responsibility, 154; com-